Bendi Benson Schrambach

EYES
TO
SEE

Experiencing God's Wonders
in All of Life's Seasons

Published by BookBaby

7905 North Route 130

Pennsauken, NJ 08110 www.bookbaby.com

All Scripture quotations, unless otherwise indicated, are from the New International Version (NIV) copyright © 1985, 1995, 2002,2008,2011 by Biblica, Inc. Used by permission of Zondervan. All rights reserved worldwide. www.zondervan.com

Edited by Hannah Mumm and Madison Smoak

Author photo by Ashley Caitlin Photography

This is a work of creative nonfiction. The author has tried to recreate events and conversations from memory, which is, of course, flawed. While all the stories in this book are true, some names have been changed for reasons of privacy.

ISBN: 978-1-09834-448-1

Printed in the United States of America

Soli Deo gloria.

CONTENTS

ACKNOWLEDGEMENTS

I would like to thank my gracious, competent, and constructive student editors, Hannah Mumm and Madison Smoak. Hannah's capable copyediting, thoughtful suggestions, and abiding merriment provided the spark that I needed to transform an idea into a manuscript. Indeed, the auspicious story of her involvement could have served as the subject matter of one of its chapters. Madison helped me to hone my prose—pointing out where stories were rushed or needed more detail, suggesting stylistic changes, and inviting me to draw out recurring themes. You ladies are true gems! Without you, this project would likely have never seen the light of day.

To my dear friends and family members, thank you for your love and support. Not a day passes that I do not recognize the blessings that you are. My life is rich because of you.

I am grateful, too, for friends and colleagues who encouraged me at some stage of this project. Tracy Bauer, Maribeth Brandt, Ina Bressler, Colette Gersten, Krista Gilbert, Shane Lanphere, Tonya Miller, Adam Neder, Lisa Setian, Jennifer Triggs, Karissa Vinal, and Jody Zadra, thank you for believing in me and with me in a God of miracles.

To my amazing children: it has been my life's greatest joy to be your mother.

After the Lord, I am most thankful for my wonderful husband. Your steadfast love, spirited humor, and winsome companionship bless and strengthen me daily.

PROLOGUE:
EYES TO SEE

Seated before the computer in our home office, I struggled to set words on the page: how to put miracles, spiritual revelations, divine appointments, small signs of the Lord's goodness into words...? It was impossible, really. Miracles are, by definition, impossible. Endeavoring to write about the many ways that the Lord had shown kindness to me would be...impossible. I sighed in discouragement.

"Oh Lord, please help me to write well," I prayed aloud. "Help me to give You glory."

A cool summer breeze blew through the open door behind me. I lifted my gaze from the computer screen to the fence bordering our yard. The replacement board that my husband had installed a few seasons back was finally beginning to blend in with the other wood slats. I hoped that our old, graying barrier would remain upright for a few more years.

Just then a quail landed atop the railing. I smiled. The Lord knew how I loved those funny dove-like birds. Though native to the area, they rarely appeared in our yard—perhaps because of the dog and, before her, the kids. In the 18 years we had lived in our home, I had never before seen a quail on our fence.

"Thank you, Lord," I whispered.

My eyes were still on the blue-gray bird when a companion leapt to join him. How very sweet, I mused. Perhaps the Lord hoped to encourage me. I had thought about writing about the many marvels that He had performed in my life for *years*. Yet the challenge of putting such things into words in a compelling, believable way had always stopped me.

I removed my hands from above the keyboard and set them in my lap momentarily. *Maybe*, I thought, just *maybe...*

And yes—a third quail appeared, and then a fourth, fifth, and sixth. Soon the rickety fence was covered with the birds—more than dozen in all—their little black crests bobbling.

My heart swelled.

"Praise you, Lord," I bowed my head. "Praise you."

The birds lingered for only a few seconds. Their little heads wriggled back and forth, eyes peering at me through the window. Then, one by one, they descended to the grassy lawn and scurried away.

Such a simple thing, birds on a fence. Nothing miraculous. But the timing of it, right when I needed encouragement, precisely when I had asked for help, suggested something of the supernatural.

Most likely, quails would not be the "sign" for you that they were for me in that moment. And while a group of iguanas balancing on our banister would've, in our climate, been much more notable—even miraculous, that phenomenon would not have inspired in *me* the same sense of God's Providence. He knew my language and, at least on this occasion, I recognized his.

The beauty of our Father is that He knows each of us personally. He knows what will bless us. We need only have eyes to see.

I have always appreciated the humanity of Peter who, after having walked on water, still denied the Lord three times. Then, before ascending to Heaven, Jesus kindly allowed Peter to declare his love for Him not once, not twice, but three times. Later, while on a roof in Joppa, Peter had a vision of a sheet containing animals considered unclean by Jewish law and heard a voice commanding him to "kill and eat."[1] *Three times.* God gave Peter the vision *three times.* You know that Peter must have grinned at that. I imagine him thinking, "Okay, Lord. I get it."

God knew Peter's language.

I heard a sermon once in which the pastor spoke of the apostle John's description of himself as "the one whom Jesus loved."[2] I had always found it an audacious assertion.

"Yet *what if*," the pastor began, "what if John just recognized this reality in a way that the others did not?" He paused to allow us to consider. "What if," he lingered again, "what if *I* am the one whom Jesus loves?" I sat up a little straighter in my seat. "What if *you* are the one whom Jesus loves? What if," he pointed to familiar faces near him, "*he* is the one and *she* is the one whom Jesus loves?"[3]

What if?

The crazy thing is: *we are* the ones whom Jesus loves (thanks be to God!). Why, then, would we doubt that an omnipotent, benevolent divinity would shower us with his kindness?

I contend that He does. Yet sometimes, in our busyness, in our rational levelheadedness, amid the noise of the world, we don't recognize these gifts for what they are. As a consequence, we miss out on the blessings that they were intended to be. We miss out, moreover, on giving God credit for His good and perfect gifts.[4]

We miss out on giving Him glory.

This book represents my feeble effort to tell of Lord's kindness, the many ways—great and small—that He has shown Himself to me.

Yet God does not love me more than He loves you. So I write also in the hope that, in reading my stories, you might begin to recognize, with the guidance of His Word and His Spirit, the many ways—great and small—that He shows his love to *you*.

May you, too, have eyes to see.

ADOPTION

"The Lord told me that we should adopt a baby!"

The Lord this, the Lord that... Joan was always talking about "the Lord." But *adopting a baby*? That seemed like a radical response to what one person perceived as the voice of God.

"And *how exactly* did the Lord *tell* you this?"

"Well," Joan considered, "it wasn't really an *audible* voice...but He did talk to me."

I scrutinized her skeptically.

"I usually hear Him best when I'm in the shower."

In the shower. How convenient. Someplace where there are no witnesses. I had already determined that these people were a bit odd...still, this took the cake.

I was seventeen and a senior in high school. Jay and Joan were the uncle and aunt of my boyfriend, Wells. They had just moved to our Montana town from North Dakota, "the Lord" having directed them to do so.

Moving was one thing, I decided, ready for a change of scenery myself. But for a couple who was struggling financially, a couple who already had two healthy children in elementary school, adopting another child was simply foolish.

Still, they were kind enough. Indeed, to this egotistical teenager, they were extremely gracious. Their house was always pleasant and welcoming.

My own home was distinctly quieter. My single mom worked a lot. And my troubled fifteen-year-old brother had been sent to spend the year with our dad and stepmom.

Wells' home, too, was oddly vacant. His single mom was never there. At her boyfriend's? At work? I never asked, and he never spoke of it. So quite naturally, we began to hang out with the lively brood at Jay and Joan's house.

When there was work to be had, Jay did construction. Joan was a happy homemaker. She baked and sewed and tidied the house while her kids were at school. She tutored, fed, and parented them when they were home. Though foreign to me, it was amiable enough.

Joan spoke often of "the Lord." I listened with a mixture of dubiousness and curiosity. Never before had I heard people talk about God as if they knew Him. Never before had I heard anyone say that God *spoke* to her in a personal way. I believed in God, but... I didn't know a God like Joan's God.

Whatever helps them through life, I surmised dismissively. At least they seemed happy.

I was busy applying to colleges, looking for scholarships, working an afterschool job. I was self-absorbed and self-centered, hardworking and determined, confident and independent. Intent on a more comfortable economic situation than I had experienced growing up, I was also completely unimpressed by what I perceived as Jay and Joan's poor financial decision-making. What kind of people would move to a new location without a job? What kind of parents would look to adopt *another* child when they barely had enough for the ones they had? I planned a different future for myself, one that included law school, financial security, and a retirement account.

Time passed and Wells' mom disappeared altogether. He moved in with Jay and Joan full time, granting me even greater access to this unusual couple. I watched them move ahead with the adoption, fill out the dossier, pray for the means to pay for it all. I heard—with ebbing measure of incredulity—stories of God's faithfulness in other arenas of their lives.

And then, a strange thing happened: I began to *want* a faith like theirs. They were unified, despite real challenges. They were generous—paying for tickets for me to attend a Christian concert with them, passing along their children's outgrown clothing items to other families in need. Perhaps most importantly, they were content, even joyful, in their daily lives.

I added some Christian colleges to my list of schools.

Spring arrived in the Northwest and then summer. Wells and I broke up and I lost my daily contact with his aunt and uncle. I worked long hours at the office supply store to save money for college. Opting for the beach over Boston, I chose Pepperdine University in Malibu, California. The Christian school affiliated with the Church of Christ's financial aid package had been the most generous. Months passed during which I did not see Jay and Joan. Then, a few days before leaving for school, I stopped to say goodbye.

Joan greeted me with her usual good cheer. Sitting at the oval oak dining table covered with mending and kids' artwork, she asked about my plans, celebrated my achievements, encouraged me in my future aspirations. I remembered why I had appreciated her so much.

Then, it was my turn to ask for updates. How was Wells? (Fine.) Any news on his mom? (With her boyfriend, somewhere.) How were the kids? (Growing.) Had Jay found more regular work? (Yes, praise the Lord!) Joan caught me up on everything.

"And what's going on with the adoption?" I asked.

"Oh, yes," Joan smiled, "the adoption." She looked down, as if searching for the answer.

"So...are you still in the process? or...or did it not get approved?" I flinched at the thought. Could "the Lord" have changed his mind?

Joan's gaze remained in her lap. Was she praying?

"We did all the paperwork, Bendi," she began, raising her eyes to meet mine. "We sent in the initial fees and everything."

I leaned closer.

"But then we realized that the Lord didn't want us to adopt a baby."

"What?!" I cried, wondering why I felt such disappointment.

Joan watched me quietly, steadily. How could she look so serene?

And what did it matter to me if the voice in the shower was real?

Joan reached her hands across the table to squeeze mine.

"We realized, Bendi, that the Lord didn't want us to take in a new *baby*," she repeated. "He wanted us to take care of *Wells*."

Tingles shot up my spine.

It was true. It was so clearly true.

I was dumbfounded.

"*Wells* is the one who needs us," Joan affirmed. "*That* is why the Lord sent us here."

OF EUNUCHS AND
FRESHMAN REJOICING

It was my first semester of college. Both out of curiosity and a need to make friends, I decided to attend the Wednesday evening chapel service on campus. The friendly faces greeting me at the door did little to appease my discomfort. I was an outsider. Unfamiliar with the order of the program, the songs, the location of different books of the Bible, I tried to mimic the actions of those around me. But it was no use. I was lost. So as the service came to a close, I prepared to slip out as inconspicuously as possible. While others lingered to visit with acquaintances old and new, I darted for the nearest exit.

"Hello," a youthful-looking student stepped in front of me, his hand extended. "I'm Michael."

"Hi, Michael," I shook his hand, taking in his well-worn clothing and mangy haircut.

The greeting accomplished, I moved to make my escape.

"How'd you like the service?"

"It was nice," I fibbed, now certain that my interloper status had not gone unnoticed.

"Well, if you have any questions..."

I had so many questions. Enrolled in a required Old Testament course, I had been reading tons of Scripture. It was all so strange, so foreign. The professor, a learned scholar, lectured as if teaching history. How was I to reconcile this erudite form of Christianity—if he was indeed a Christian—with the faith of Jay and Joan?

"Or if you ever want to talk about any of this..." Michael continued. He sounded sincere.

"I *do* have some questions."

We set a time to get together the following week. An aspiring pastor, Michael asked me to read passages of the Bible in preparation for our discussions. We began with the Gospel of John, moved on to Paul's letter to the Romans, and then to Luke's account of the First Century Church in Acts.

Michael and I met weekly throughout the semester. Little by little, I was able to piece together a vague notion of the biblical story, from Eden to Calvary. I returned to the Wednesday evening gatherings where I met other Christians—Darlene and Chantal and Greg—who, like Michael, made efforts to befriend me notwithstanding my own well-worn clothing and mangy haircut. Eventually, I even began to recognize some of the prophecies about Christ in my Old Testament class. Some, like this one, were quite compelling:

> But he was pierced for our transgressions, he was crushed for our iniquities; the punishment that brought us peace was on him, and by his wounds we are healed. We all, like sheep, have gone astray, each of us has turned to our own way; and the Lord has laid on him the iniquity of us all. He was oppressed and afflicted, yet he did not open his mouth; he was led like a lamb to the slaughter, and as a sheep before its shearers is silent, so he did not open his mouth.[1]

How, I thought, could this have been written 700 years *before* Jesus?

Barriers to my belief remained, however. Working through the Scriptures with Michael, I was ever-more aware that faith in Christ would necessitate changes to my moral code, concrete alterations of my actions and pursuits. I wasn't sure that I wanted that part of Christianity.

The end of the term approached. I would be going home for Christmas, spending time with my unbelieving family, reconnecting with high school friends, and—most likely—repeating old habits and behaviors. Not having been home all semester, I looked forward to being among friends, to the familiar, to being known.

Final exams were winding down when Michael called.

"Hey, Bendi. I need to talk to you."

"Okay. Do you wanna meet?"

"No."

Silence.

"Hello?"

"I'm here."

"You okay?" I wondered if Michael had failed an exam.

"Yeah, I'm fine." He took a big breath. "I just, um, I just wanted to let you know that I'm not going to be able to return in the spring."

"Oh, Michael, I'm sorry." I knew that he struggled financially. "So, will you take a semester off and come back in the fall?"

"No." He sounded definitive. "I won't be coming back."

I gasped. It felt like someone had pulled the rug out from underneath me. Michael had been a sort of lifeline. Without him, I would be adrift again, without grounding, without a compass. For while Michael was not *God*, he was trying so very earnestly to introduce me to Him.

"Take care, Bendi."

"Thanks, Michael." I swallowed. "Thank you for everything."

The phone clicked and he was gone.

Alone in my dorm room, I sank onto my bed, curled up on my side, and prayed.

I had never understood the metaphor before then. But there it was, right before me. Would I make the "leap of faith?" Would I put my confidence in Jesus, submit to His plan for my life? Or would I continue on the path that I had walked until then with relative success? The familiar was easy, known—even promising from the world's perspective. Belief was unfamiliar, unknown. And while I ultimately came to appreciate Joan—her joy, her peace, her worshipful spirit, I had long looked down upon what I had perceived as naivety and blind faith.

Would others consider me naive and foolish?

Did that matter if Jesus really was God?

I picked up the phone.

"Hello?"

"Hi, Michael. It's Bendi."

"Hello, again."

"Hey, I was thinking...about all the stuff that we've been talking about..."

In the beginning was the Word, and the Word was with God and the Word was God.[2]

"Yeah?"

Therefore, I urge you, brothers and sisters, in view of God's mercy, to offer your bodies as a living sacrifice, holy and pleasing to God.[3]

Holding the phone in my trembling hand, I thought of Philip, led by the Spirit to speak to the Ethiopian eunuch about the same chapter from Isaiah that had so marked me in my Old Testament class.

Now an angel of the Lord said to Philip, "Go south to the road— the desert road—that goes down from Jerusalem to Gaza." So he started out, and on his way he met an Ethiopian eunuch, an important official...This man had gone to Jerusalem to worship, and on his way home was sitting in his chariot reading the Book of Isaiah the prophet. The Spirit told Philip, "Go to that chariot and stay near it."

Then Philip ran up to the chariot and heard the man reading Isaiah the prophet.

"Do you understand what you are reading?" Philip asked.

"How can I," he said, "unless someone explains it to me?" So he invited Philip to come up and sit with him.

This is the passage of Scripture the eunuch was reading:

"He was led like a sheep to the slaughter, and as a lamb before its shearer is silent, so he did not open his mouth. In his humiliation he was deprived of justice. Who can speak of his descendants? For his life was taken from the earth."

The eunuch asked Philip, "Tell me, please, who is the prophet talking about, himself or someone else?" Then Philip began with that very passage of Scripture and told him the good news about Jesus.

As they traveled along the road, they came to some water and the eunuch said, "Look, here is water. What can stand in the way of my being baptized?" And he gave orders to stop the chariot. Then both Philip and the eunuch went down into the water and Philip baptized him.[4]

My heart pounded in my chest.

"And, um...I'm ready to accept Christ. Will you baptize me, Michael?"

There was a long silence on the other end of the phone.

"That's wonderful news, Bendi." I could hear the smile in Michael's voice. "I would be honored to baptize you."

We made plans for that very afternoon. And though Michael encouraged me to invite others, it was only God and Michael in attendance when I was buried with Christ and raised as a new creation. Michael, who walked into the ocean with me—fully dressed because he thought that that was how Jesus would have done it—gave me a small Bible to commemorate the event.

And when we came up out of the water, the Spirit of the Lord suddenly took Michael away, and I did not see him again, but went on my way rejoicing.[5]

BLESSED

A freshly-cut pine was strung with popcorn strings and bestrewn with homemade Christmas ornaments when I arrived at Jay and Joan's to tell them about my decision for Christ. They were thrilled. Over the same busy dining room table, we caught up on the events of the preceding months. The countertop radio hummed Christian instrumental worship songs as they laid their hands on me to pray. Then, as the visit drew to a close, Joan announced their upcoming plans.

"Bendi, we probably won't be here when you return this summer. With Wells graduating, we're moving back to North Dakota."

"Oh, I'm sorry to hear that."

"We've enjoyed it here, but our mission is complete. We want to go home."

"I understand."

We hugged, exchanged addresses, and promised to keep in touch.

Returned to campus after the holidays, I was surprised to find a package in my student mailbox. The senders: Jay and Joan. Ever-generous;

ever-thoughtful. Closing the mail compartment with my key, I found a quiet spot away from the foot traffic of the cafeteria to open my present.

The parcel was about two inches thick. A journal? A devotional book? Removing the brown outer wrap, I read the description on the box: "Personalized Name Plaque."

Ugh.

I had mixed feelings about my name, whose uniqueness had always been a topic of conversation. Introducing myself, I inevitability had to explain its origin: "My dad, who had had a boy name all picked out, was looking for something unique. 'Let's call her *Bendi...Bendi Benson*. With a name like that, she can swing a bat and be a cheerleader, too.'"

Growing up, I had endured significant teasing—from rhymes and ribbing ("Are you flexible?") to a rousing song about my name: "Bendi, do you bend? Bendi, do you bend? Bendi, do you bend, do you bend, bend, bend?"

I shuddered at the memory.

And yet, here was a gift celebrating my name. Oh well, I thought. It was a nice gesture. I took comfort in the fact that Jay and Joan would not likely be visiting my dorm room any time soon to discover whether or not the plaque was on display.

Opening one flap of the cardboard, I pulled out the tissue-covered plank. Then setting the box aside, I unwound the paper to examine their offering. It was a solid beveled board about five inches tall and nine inches wide with a hook on one side for hanging. A tan plastic laminate covered its face. On it, in large black font, was my name, its meaning, and a Bible verse. I wondered if Jay and Joan had chosen the scripture from Jeremiah: "'For I know the plans I have for you,' declares the Lord, 'plans to prosper you and not to harm you, plans to give you hope and a future.'"[1]

What a beautiful promise.

It was, I realized, the first time that I had ever reflected on the *meaning* of names. I had never before considered that there might be any inherent significance in the order of the letters—just that a child was born and a name assigned. We called Joan, "Joan," and Jay, "Jay," like we called a flower, "flower." Within each language, people just tacitly agreed to use the same designations for objects in order to ensure communication. I had studied a little Spanish in high school and was currently studying Italian and French. It helped that they all shared Latin roots.

Looking at the plaque, I recognized—again, for the first time—the Latin radicles in my name: "Ben" from the Latin "běnědīco" (the Italian "benedire"; the French "bénir"); "di" from the Latin "deus" (the Italian "dio"; the French "dieu").

How had I never seen it before? I thought numbly. What a sweet surprise.

"Bendi," the plaque declared. "Blessed by God."

SWEET MERCY

Ababy Christian, I was trying to grow up in the faith. To that end, I had
signed up for a class at my church, a nondenominational evangelical
house of worship in Santa Monica that I attended with several of my university peers. The subject that day was the prophet Isaiah's vision of the Lord:

> In the year that King Uzziah died, I saw the Lord, high and
> exalted, seated on a throne; and the train of his robe filled the
> temple. Above him were seraphim, each with six wings: With
> two wings they covered their faces, with two they covered their
> feet, and with two they were flying. And they were calling to
> one another:
>
> "Holy, holy, holy is the Lord Almighty; the whole earth is full
> of his glory."
>
> At the sound of their voices the doorposts and thresholds shook
> and the temple was filled with smoke.
>
> "Woe to me!" I cried. "I am ruined! For I am a man of unclean
> lips, and I live among a people of unclean lips, and my eyes have
> seen the King, the Lord Almighty."

Then one of the seraphim flew to me with a live coal in his hand, which he had taken with tongs from the altar. With it he touched my mouth and said, "See, this has touched your lips; your guilt is taken away and your sin atoned for."

Then I heard the voice of the Lord saying, "Whom shall I send? And who will go for us?"

And I said, "Here am I. Send me!"[1]

The church leader talked about the seraphim's worship, inspired—compelled—by the holiness of God. He discussed the significance of three, number of perfection: Father, Son and Holy Spirit; sun, moon and stars; "Holy, holy, holy." He pointed out Isaiah's dramatic response, like that of any person recorded in the Bible who became aware of God's presence. In light of Divine Majesty, the prophet expresses contrition, sorrow, repentance for his vileness. The pastor explained, finally, the symbolism of the live coal taken from the altar granting pardon to the prophet: God's mercy—unmerited and undeserved.

I was lost in thought while returning to campus on Pacific Coast Highway. With the windows down in my early 80s model Honda Accord, I took in the salty ocean air. The churning waves on the shore to my left, nearly imperceptible in the obscurity of night, stirred and soothed me.

How could something so powerful be so peaceful? The mystery.

Isaiah had a revelation of God's power, a vision that brought him to his knees. He saw the God who created the oceans.

Marvelous.

And while the prophet had evidently sought after the God of Abraham, Isaac, and Jacob, his was a secondary role in the celestial encounter. For the One who gave the vision, the One who atoned, and the One who commissioned was God.

The crests of the waves shimmered in the light of the moon. Bubbling. Rhapsodic. Relentless.

All my life, I had worked hard to achieve, to be successful, to earn...

What? I considered. My salvation? Maybe. To some meager degree, I *had* sought to please God—even when I didn't know Him. I had always sensed that He was there...*somewhere*.

But good grades didn't matter to God. Did they? Making the softball team didn't matter to God. Being good at golf and excelling at billiard and aspiring to go to law school didn't matter to God.

And then it hit me. Like a crashing wave.

My hard work, my achievements, my striving had *not* been aimed at winning God's approval. They had, instead, been an effort to please...*my dad*.

"I made ten assists at the game last night!"

"That's great, honey. How many points did you score?"

"I got third in the city talent show!"

"That's neat! Who got first?"

"I have a 3.9 GPA, Dad!"

"What'd you get the B in, honey? What do you need to do to get an A next time?"

Success had been my effort to win Dad's approval—or at least, to get his attention. His parenting presence during my youth had been minimal. Work and his new family had taken much of his time. Yet even when I did have something "grand" to announce, it always seemed like there was more to do, ways to improve.

It was never enough.

I didn't blame him. He had not had a great role model for a father. And I knew that he loved me.

Still, I strove and I strove. And I had begun to transfer this mentality to my relationship with God.

And I didn't need to do it anymore.

A wave of emotion washed over me.

That was it! Jesus had done everything! I didn't need to do *anything* to gain his approval. Indeed, I *couldn't* "earn" my salvation—not by scoring points or succeeding at school or even being a "good" Christian—whatever that meant. Because of the cross, my perfect Heavenly Father accepted me *just as I was.*

I pulled the car to the side of the road, leaned over the steering wheel, and wept.

So many years of striving. So many wasted years.

The tide rolled in unfettered. The sound of mercy. Deliverance. *Relief.*

LIFE IN COLOR

The world changed when I accepted Christ. With the veils removed from my eyes,[1] I recognized for the first time the Christians whose paths had crossed mine while I was still living in my own sufficiency. I could see how the Lord had protected and drawn me to Him since, around age 10, I had asked Jesus into my heart when invited to church by a classmate whose name I couldn't even remember (thank you!). Yet without anyone to disciple me, I had floundered and lost my way. I recalled a journal entry from my 15-year-old self seeking direction that I now knew only the Lord could provide. And I marveled at the majesty of creation: oceans and lakes, elephants and dolphins, sequoias and roses, hummingbirds and butterflies.

I had always loved butterflies. Growing up in Western Montana, these miniature masterpieces were a welcome sign of spring. Since springtime meant longer days, warmer temperatures, more sunshine and, eventually, summer vacation from school, butterflies came to symbolize all that was good and beautiful and fleeting. In California where I attended college, butterflies were in greater abundance. Still, following my conversion, I was convinced that the Lord had graced my path with these floating fairies on the most poignant of occasions. Like the song that came on the radio at the perfect moment, the long-lost friend who called at just the right time, the Word that cut to the quick, the Lord had seemed to encourage and bless me with butterflies.

It was to be my first summer home after accepting Christ. Though growing in my faith, I was nervous to return to my old stomping grounds. Numerous friends and family members had yet to meet the newly-saved version of Bendi. Georgia was the exception.

Beautiful and bubbly and bright, Georgia had witnessed to me in high school. While many of those seeds had fallen onto hardened ground,[2] they were not forgotten when, in anticipation of my homecoming, I reached out to her seeking Christian fellowship for my summer sojourn in the Northwest. Georgia enthusiastically agreed.

Both lovers of hikes and nature, we determined one morning to admire the Lord's handiwork from the impressive Ch-paa-qn Peak. We set out early, intent on a climb and some devotional time before breakfast.

At nearly 8,000 feet in elevation, Ch-paa-qn Peak's pointed summit stood tall amongst the Rocky Mountains, rising 4,000 feet above its neighbors in the northern Bitterroot Range. The Salish name of this symmetrical pyramid signified "gray, treeless mountain top," a feature which made it popular in the winter with backcountry skiers.

Ours was the only car in the parking lot when we arrived at the trailhead, elevation 6,229 feet. We were confident that the five and a half mile round trip would take us about two hours. We donned sweatshirts in brisk morning air and began our ascent with faith that God had something to reveal to us that day.

Striding up the well-marked trail, Georgia and I chatted about school and boys, family and friends, our plans and dreams for the future. We stopped every so often to appreciate a wildflower, breathe in the mountain air, and goggle at the valleys below. As the sun, now climbed out from behind the tall mountains, warmed our limbs, we tied our sweatshirts around our waists.

I began to regret having left our water bottles in the car.

An hour in, the trail dissipated. While we playfully pushed back branches and jumped over fallen pines, scratches began to appear on my face, arms, and legs. Unstable rocks gave way, causing my ankles to strain with effort.

Still, we had the joy of the Lord. We had each other. We had the energy of youth.

Finally above the treeline, we climbed atop ashen rock. We continued upward, onward until, at last, we arrived at the summit.

There were mountains and rivers and trees as far as the eye could see. I had taken it all for granted as a child. Now, I stood in awe.

"He made the earth by His power," wrote the prophet Jeremiah. "He founded the world by His wisdom and stretched out the heavens by his understanding."[3]"The Lord is the great God, the great King above all gods. In his hand are the depths of the earth, and the mountain peaks belong to him."[4]

Georgia and I took in the 360 degree views. We commended the Lord's creativity. We celebrated his splendor.

Then after resting for several moments in silent reverence, we were interrupted, in the end, by the rumblings of our empty stomachs.

"Shall we go?"

The sun kissed our noses and warmed our backs as we descended the first several hundred yards on what appeared to be lava rock, which covered the entire apex of the mountain. The arid landscape, with its pale color and barrenness, resembled a vast desert. At last, we found shelter again in the coolness of the timber.

We paused to get our bearings. No path was evident.

"I think it's this way."

With a little less bounce in our step, we continued downward.

Our conversation returned to the mundane—our summer jobs, living arrangements, exercise routines. We stepped more gingerly to avoid tree roots. We defended ourselves and each other with greater care from pummeling branches. I was looking forward to a large quantity of water and a big breakfast.

"Does this look familiar to you?"

"Not really. But it all kind of looks the same, doesn't it?"

"We must be getting close."

But time passed and the woods just got thicker. Though I tried not to panic, there was no denying the growing sense of malaise.

"Dear God," Georgia stopped to pray, "please guide us."

"Amen."

More trees with no sign of a path. Our pace had slowed to a crawl, or rather, we were nearly crawling in the thick brush. I was exhausted. We had been hiking for hours and the trail was nowhere in sight.

Now and then, a glimmer of sunshine would find its way through the deep woods to hearten us. I looked up to draw strength from its radiance.

"Georgia," I began, "maybe we need to go back up." Though I dreaded the idea of climbing again, our current efforts did not seem to be working. "Maybe we need to go back up so we can have a better perspective, see things more clearly."

My friend stopped to consider. "I think you're right."

So with a breath of courage, we turned back toward the summit.

For the next several minutes, we spoke little. Trying to conserve our energy, we focused on the essentials: good foot placement, ready hands to steady us if we fell, a positive attitude. We plodded on, upward, until finally we emerged again from the somber woods of the mighty mountain. The sun was hot on our now-perspiring skin.

"Whattya think?"

"We still can't see much from here."

"We need to get higher."

A nod. A deep breath. And up we went.

Judging by the sun, it was now near midday. What we had planned as a two hour adventure had turned into three—and we were not yet returned to the peak where we would recommence our descent. In the arid alpine air, my throat was parched; my feet, heavy; and my mind, distraught. I thought of stories I had seen in the paper about hikers who had disappeared into the mountains to face frostbite or animals or death.

What had we been thinking to hike on empty stomachs without water and food?

Looking up again, I prayed for peace. I asked God for strength. I started to lock my knees between steps.

Gradually, an idea began to emerge.

"Georgia," I mused aloud, "maybe *that* is the lesson that God's trying to show us today."

"What's that?" My friend paused to look at me.

"Maybe He wants to remind us that we always need to look *up*, to *Him,* for direction." Though I was still formulating my theory, it sounded right. "When we are lost or without direction, when we can't see clearly, we need to look 'up.'" I smiled sheepishly at the corniness of it.

Georgia laughed in approval.

"A good lesson," she agreed.

Arriving finally at the summit, again, we only quickly took in the grandeur. Then, following an earnest prayer for direction, we set our course. We descended silently this time, concentrating on our surroundings, endeavoring to master the discomfort of our physical needs. We were again nearing the treeline when Georgia stopped.

"Do you hear that?"

I tipped my head to one side. A warm breeze blew across my dusty face. Crickets.

"Over there!" Georgia pointed excitedly.

Finally, I heard it—human conversation. I sighed with relief.

More quickly now, we made our way toward the voices. "Hello! Hello!" Georgia called kindly, urgently.

And then we saw them, our unlikely saviors. The ascending hikers pointed us to the trail, just a few dozen yards to the right of where we had initially descended. Then, thanking them, we ran-walked to the car.

Tired and relieved but contented, we gulped our water, rinsed our faces, and reminisced on the lesson that the Lord had shown us. For the inspiration and the enlightenment, it had been worth the trip.

At last, we turned out of the parking area in the direction of what would now be a late lunch. Basking in the sweet silence of friendship, I watched as the dirt road coughed up gravel and dust.

Suddenly, the air was filled with color. It flew up from beneath the hood of the car as if we had just landed on a rainbow pallet of chalk.

Georgia stopped the vehicle. We stared, incredulous.

"This is crazy."

"I've never seen anything like it."

"*Amaaazing!*"

Twisting our heads in all directions, we tried to take it in. A magical vision. Like an enchanted scene from a movie. A full-color picture book come to life.

For before, behind, all around us, there were butterflies! *Hundreds and hundreds* of butterflies!

SNEAKING OUT 2.0

I met a man. While on a summer exchange program in Paris. And the course my life was forever changed.

Five weeks later, Daniel wistfully drove me to the airport for my trip home. He had already made arrangements to come to the States at the end of the summer and make the trek with me from Montana to California. I planned to spend my senior year of college devising a way for us to be together following my graduation.

In August, Daniel arrived to meet my parents. (Mom was smitten; Dad, reticent.)

He came for another visit in October. During that trip that, after a particularly euphoric run on Old Malibu Road, he asked me to marry him. And I accepted. Given my graduation at the end of April, we set a wedding date for the beginning of May.

My parents were a bit concerned.

"Are you sure he doesn't just want a green card?"

"There's no rush!"

"Why don't you just live together?"

Theirs was a different worldview than ours. There was also the matter of visas and green cards, and of permission to live in a country of which one was not a citizen. Marriage, we were convinced, was the solution to it all.

We spent Christmas in Montana. Upon our return to California for my last semester, Daniel purchased a 31' ketch (sailboat), which he moored in Marina del Rey. While I attended classes, worked part-time, and studied, he prepared the sailboat for our honeymoon voyage "around the world."

Wedding planning was conducted via phone with the help of my parents and step-mother. Though terrified that I was making a colossal mistake, they kindly kept their mouths shut. With no wedding party on Daniel's side and doubts that his family would be in attendance, it was to be an atypical affair. We invited my large extended tribe and many friends. A group of my classmates also committed to blessing us with their presence. So following graduation, our small caravan headed north for the nuptials.

We were working on final details and trying to entertain our friends in Montana. Daniel asked to speak with me in private. There was real concern on his face.

"What's wrong?" I asked once we were out of earshot of the others. "Are you alright?"

"I just noticed the expiration date of my visa," he announced. "It's tomorrow."

"What does that mean?"

"It means that I'll be in the country illegally after that." He took my hands in his. "It means that they might not give me a green card to work. It means that, when we return from our sailing trip, they might not let me back into the country."

"Oh, no," my stomach sank. "What should we do?"

We stood in silence for several moments, the laughter of friends in the other room unable to lighten the heaviness of the air around us.

We certainly wanted to respect the laws of the land... and, still months away from departing on our boat trip, we needed Daniel to work... and, while we would consider living in France for a season, we didn't want to make it impossible to ever live in the States again.

There was, upon reflection, only one good option.

"We could go to the city hall to get married," I suggested. We already had all the necessary documents for the marriage certificate.

"How does that work?"

"Well, I'm not really sure...but I don't think we need an appointment."

"When?"

"We could go... *now*, I guess...?" Daniel squeezed my hands and nodded, relief washing over his face.

"But what about the church wedding?" he asked quietly.

"We'll do that, too," I assured him. We certainly couldn't—shouldn't—cancel everything at this point. "Let's just not tell anyone for a while. Okay?"

"Of course," he smiled.

We invented a pretext to excuse ourselves and made our way to city hall. My head was spinning.

Were we really doing this?

Should we be doing this?

Yes, we had planned on getting married, we *would* be getting married in a few short days. Yet this felt secretive (since it was!), and even lonely. I had been looking forward to joining our lives in front of family and friends. Both Mom and Dad would walk me down the aisle. My brothers would serve as ushers and ring bearer. I would wear my grandmother's pearls and a dress made for me by the mother of my high school chum, Shelly. Georgia and Mr. Chamberlain, my favorite high school teacher, would provide musical accompaniment. And Darlene would read this beautiful passage from Ecclesiastes:

Two are better than one, because they have a good return for their labor: If either of them falls down, one can help the other up. But pity anyone who falls and has no one to help them up. Also, if two lie down together, they will keep warm. But how can one keep warm alone? Though one may be overpowered, two can defend themselves. A cord of three strands is not quickly broken.[1]

We were counting on God to be the third strand.

Daniel was blissfully ignorant of all this. He didn't need all the bells and whistles. Truth be told, he preferred the idea of it being just the two of us.

We arrived at the county offices and, hand-in-hand, entered the door of the Clerk of District Court. My heart raced.

"Hello," I addressed a woman behind the desk. "Um, we'd like to get married."

"Pardon me?"

"We'd like to get married. Here. Today. Can we do that?"

The woman's eyebrows raised curiously. "You'd like to get married *here?*" she repeated.

We nodded our heads. "Yes."

"I'll have to check into that." She rose from her chair and walked around to what were apparently the judges' chambers. We could hear her asking about our request, heard a male voice reply, with evident surprise, in the affirmative. She returned with some paperwork.

"And where are your witnesses?" she asked as I turned in the forms.

"We don't have any witnesses," I admitted.

A roar of silence engulfed the room.

What would we do now?

"Could you be our witnesses?" Daniel suggested, pointing to the woman and her coworker.

They looked at each other quizzically, contemplating, and then shrugged.

"I don't see why not!" the first woman replied. She smiled as she carried the paperwork back to the justice of the peace.

The voice reached me before the woman had returned to the front office.

"Bendi?! Bendi Benson, is that *you!?*"

The judge walked out of his chambers holding our application in one hand, his reading glasses in the other.

"Mr. Morris!" I cried, shocked to see my childhood friend's father emerge from the judges' chambers. Mr. Morris had also been the one who had caught Jenny and me sneaking out to Kari's house in seventh grade. It had been my bright idea. Mr. Morris had made quite a fuss of it. Jenny and I had not been allowed to hang out much after that.

I was mortified.

How would I explain this?

A flood of emotions pulsed through me as Mr. Morris approached, extended his arms, and pulled me in for a gentle hug.

"It is so *good* to see you, Bendi," he murmured earnestly. "And what a wonderful occasion brings you here!" He turned then to Daniel and extended his hand. "Bendi was a dear friend of our daughter, Jennifer," he said.

"Nice to meet you, sir." Daniel shook his hand.

Mr. Morris scrutinized him as any father would—taking in the firmness of his handshake, the steadiness of his eye contact, the sincerity of his tone. Nodding mildly in approval, the judge turned back to me.

"So, you want to get *married*," he grinned.

Thankful for the warm reception, I confessed all. Explaining our predicament, I begged Judge Morris not to tell my parents. He graciously agreed. In fact, my friend's father seemed genuinely happy to take part in our project. As the desk clerk prepared the paperwork, we talked about his children, my family, our plans.

"Well, it looks like we're ready here," Judge Morris announced finally, beckoning to the office workers. "Shall we?" He pointed to the courtroom, just across the hall. I inhaled deeply and turned to my dapper fiancé. He smiled, squeezing my hands again affectionately. We followed Judge Morris and our witnesses into the courtroom.

The ceremony was short but sweet. Judge Morris spoke to us as would a parent—with fondness and affection. Our witnesses, likewise, exuded only hopefulness and good cheer. They hugged us good-naturedly before signing the wedding certificate.

Daniel never let go of my hands. His face, fixed on mine, shone with confidence. Tears glistened in his eyes as Judge Morris pronounced us "man and wife."

And just like that, we were married.

WE CAN MAKE OUR PLANS[1]

Aplanner, I had decided that we would have kids about five years after getting married. That's what I said to anyone who asked, anyway. Truth be told, Daniel and I hadn't talked much about children. (Engaged after only four months while living on different continents, we hadn't talked about a lot of things.) There was plenty of time for kids, I assured myself. We would decide on the proper time for children in a future that seemed about five years hence.

Following the wedding, we returned to Marina del Rey to undertake the final preparations for our boat cruise. A few short months later, we set out on our maiden voyage aboard our little sailboat. We christened her *Butterfly*.

Just before our departure, a friend gave us a small plaque that displayed what he called, "the sailor's prayer." The credo read, in part, "O God, Thy sea is so great and my boat is so small."

The orison was correct! Against the roar of the waves and might of the wind, atop the vast, mysterious blue, we quickly recognized our minuteness in the whole scheme of things. One slight error in navigation could smash our hull against a coral reef. The vigorous tail slapping of a migrating humpback whale, nearly twice our size, could capsize our little ship far from the security of land. An unexpected storm or even a large breaking wave could bring our boat, even our lives, to a sudden watery end. I realized for the first time how fragile we really were.

And I saw, anew and afresh, the greatness of our God: "He alone stretches out the heavens and treads on the waves of the sea. He is the Maker of the Bear and Orion, the Pleiades and the constellations of the south. He performs wonders that cannot be fathomed, miracles that cannot be counted."[2] Pods of dolphins escorted us, romping playfully near our bow. Pacific black sea turtles who—unlike the dolphins—were uninterested in our coos of admiration, bobbed conspicuously on the tide. Bioluminescent plankton illuminated the night sea with their radiance. It was amazing, awe-inspiring, breathtaking.

It was also strangely difficult. We began our life as a married couple in somewhat precarious circumstances. We needed each other simply to survive. Confined to a living area of about 200 square feet, Daniel and I were together 24 hours a day, seven days a week. There was no place to go after an argument, no means—without satellite phones or even a Ham radio—to easily call a friend or family member to vent or just share life.

I was also intensely restless. Having just graduated from college, I was ready to take on the world. Yet, there I was, stuck on boat somewhere off the coast of Central America. I felt like I was wasting time. I read voluminously from books obtained through the cruiser network. I played with our kitty-cat cruising companion. Mostly, I looked forward to our next chapter on terra firma.

Our longest crossing was to be between El Salvador and Costa Rica—five days and four nights without touching land. This, we had decided, would be the best means to avoid the violence and political chaos plaguing the region. We divided each day into three-hour shifts during which the person on duty was expected to scrutinize the skyline at least every 20 minutes. That was the approximate span it took for a commercial cruise liner on the horizon to reach and potentially ravage a vessel—us!—if in its pathway.

My preferred shift was the first tour of the morning: 3 a.m.-6 a.m. As the sky turned from black to brown to purple, I thanked the Lord that the light overcame the darkness.[3] I thanked Him for his faithfulness, which was new every morning.[4] I thanked Him for our safety and for the hope and promise of the new day.

It was during this first tour of the morning of our second day asea that I saw a little powerboat near the shoreline of Nicaragua. There looked to be three or four people in the craft, which—I could now detect—was moving out to sea. After a few minutes, it became clear that they were coming directly towards us.

"Daniel!" I called from the comfortable nest I had made in the cockpit. "Daniel, could you come here?"

Hearing no response, I left the helm to awaken my beloved.

"A boat is coming this way!"

"So?"

"So, maybe they're pirates."

"There are no pirates here," Daniel sighed. Still, he roused himself to follow me above deck.

The foreign vessel was closer now. Four figures stood in the traditional fishing boat with large outboard engine. On their faces were ski masks.

"Get below," Daniel insisted. Immediately, he began searching for some means of defense against a potential attack: a flare gun, gasoline...

Seeing that I had not descended into the living area, Daniel urged again: "Go below deck! I'll take care of it." His tone was urgent.

"Why?" I pleaded, my heart pounding. "I should be with you."

Daniel swallowed. He looked out again to the uninvited visitors. They were very near now—about 400 yards and counting. He had no time to argue. Daniel braced himself in the cockpit for whatever would come.

Would this be how it all ended? "Newlyweds disappear somewhere in the Pacific. The couple, believed to have been aboard a 31' ketch, was last seen in San Diego in January." I thought of my poor mother. She had always believed in Daniel. *Would she think me abducted?*

Did it matter now?

I positioned myself behind my husband and prayed.

The boat never veered from our direction. It came at us, moreover, at full speed. I could feel Daniel's arm tense as he began to lift the flare gun when, about 100 yards from our bow, the passengers removed the dark masks from their faces. And there in the cool dawn of the morning shone the visages of four smiling young men—boys really. They waved at us affably while checking out our unfamiliar vessel. Then, still smiling and waving, they turned and continued their course out to sea. We were left rolling in their wake.

Amazing. Awe-inspiring. Breathtaking.

Daniel and I made it through the Panama Canal before returning to the States, a seven month voyage in all. By then, it was hurricane season and the summer of my brother's wedding. It was also time to begin repaying my student loans. With the cat, who ever-after walked like a seasoned sailor, we moved in with my mom and live-in boyfriend, Paul, and slept à *deux* in my childhood twin-sized bed. Accompanied by a steady stream of classic country—Willie and Waylon and George—we cooked together; we snowmobiled and double-dated at restaurants. With much eagerness, I began applying to graduate programs. Daniel found work in the restaurant industry and I returned to the office-supply store where I started in accounts receivable. Each morning, in my same baby blue Honda, I dropped my husband at the diner where he worked until three, at which time I took my lunch break so as to shuttle him from his first gig to his second at a downtown pub. This, we did for six months.

Then, upon hearing of a big earthquake in Southern California, Daniel called to check on some friends and Jean-Claude invited him to help open a restaurant. It sounded like a promising new beginning. So we loaded up our chariot with our few worldly belongings and headed back to Los Angeles.

We spent several months hemorrhaging rent payments on a beachside studio until Daniel decided that we should purchase another boat on which we could live. He found our 43 foot motoryacht, procured via three credit cards, at an auction of repossessed boats. We named her *Renaissance*, French for "rebirth."

At dinner with friends one night—an Italian place near the pier at the end of Washington Boulevard—the subject of children arose again. We had met Paco, owner of neighboring sailboat *Alleycat*, while preparing *Butterfly* for our honeymoon voyage. Arcy had arrived sometime between our departure and return to Marina del Rey. Now some four years later, Paco and Daniel competed in weekly regattas in the marina. The men were debating the wisdom of a particular nautical maneuver when Arcy leaned across the table toward me.

"So, what are you guys thinking about kids?"

I wondered if Arcy was getting the itch. I had heard of the phenomenon, though had not yet experienced it. Then again, Arcy was probably a few years older than me.

"Oh, I don't know," I admitted. "Maybe five years?" It was my standard reply. With my Master's exams scheduled for the end of the academic year, it was not the season for children. Five years seemed like a reasonable amount of time for me to finish my doctoral coursework and write a dissertation. At least, I hoped it was.

"What about you guys?"

"Yeah, five years sounds about right."

It was agreed, then. And how fun it would be to have children of similar ages! We called it a "plan."

A week later, Arcy phoned with the news.

"I'm pregnant!"

"Wow!" I gushed, feeling as if I had dodged a bullet. "How wonderful!" And how crazy to think that we had only just discussed it.

"The funny thing is," Arcy continued, "I was pregnant when we had dinner and didn't know it!"

Funny, I thought. *Indeed.*

Just days later we learned that I, too, was very unexpectedly, very unpreparedly pregnant. In fact, a visit to the doctor confirmed that my pregnancy was even more advanced than my friend's.

Surprise, excitement, fear, frustration...so many emotions filled my heart and mind. For weeks after learning of my condition, I didn't even want to share the news with others because I was unable to pretend to be happy about it. My carefully laid plans were crumbling.

How was I going to finish my Masters with a baby due a month before the scheduled exams?

How would we care for a child with me in school and Daniel working two jobs?

How would we pay for it all?

Daniel, on the contrary, was thrilled.

"My wife's pregnant!" he beckoned to cars at the stoplight.

"We're going to have a baby!" he raved to fellow racers at the regattas.

"I'm going to be a dad!" he blathered to our neighbors on the docks.

The Lord blessed me with his enthusiasm. The Lord also blessed me with several months to get used to the idea. And little by little, I did.

Our beloved baby boy came into the world on a bright sunny day in late April. It was amazing. Awe-inspiring. Breathtaking.

Our first child arrived exactly *five years* after our wedding date.

Five years and a day.

LIFE

We had prayed for our child while he was still in the womb. Yet even the months of knowing and praying for him could not have prepared me for the overwhelming emotion of that first moment the doctor laid him in my arms. He was so beautiful. Blue and purple, cone-headed, with dark hair and an enormous mouth. He let out his first cry and the earth stopped.

Immediately, I realized that I could do nothing to protect him anymore. He had been safe inside of me. While he was in my belly, I could love and pray for him and go to the doctor to check on him. I ate well and slept well...all with him in mind. Suddenly, he entered a world in which I could control almost nothing. Suddenly, my actions alone could not keep him from harm. The world had forever changed.

Daniel couldn't take his eyes off of him. He held him as if he were the finest crystal, rocked him with infinite tenderness. For one of the rare moments in his life, my husband was without words.

Together in the delivery room, we prayed for our son. We prayed that God would bless him with knowledge of Him as Lord and Savior at a young age. We prayed that He would protect him with his angels and give him his joy and his peace. Almost as importantly, it seemed, we prayed for us—that God would give us the wisdom to raise him in his ways.

Daniel and I could barely believe that anyone would allow us to leave the hospital with him. We had no idea what we were doing. One needs a license to drive a car, a degree to teach. The oversight of a human life, one would think, would necessitate some modicum of instruction. But no—a car seat was all that was required.

Fortunately for us all, my mother and grandmother came to visit when Alexander was only a week old. Their experienced arms held and rocked him. Their soothing voices calmed him. Their delight in him was contagious.

Even more than their proposed techniques on burping, swaddling, and dressing him, however, were their perspectives, seasoned and wise, that blessed me. His spit-ups were not always indigestion, but overconsumption. His whimper was not always distress, but lung exertion. This season of exhaustion would not be interminable, but fleeting. They smiled when his little hand squeezed their fingers, laughed at his strange noises, cried with him on the occasion of his first shots. Their company and mirth were of great comfort to me.

Only a few times in my life had I experienced what might have been called a revelation. Having a baby, being a mother, granted a new one. Indeed, I couldn't believe that I had never seen it before. It was the cycle of life. Somehow, in some non-spiritual way, through children we gain "immortality." I saw this in the eyes of my mother and grandmother. My child represented hope and promise for a future that they might not ever see. We would, in effect, "live on" through him.

Was that why we found him so beautiful?

Thus, in the blink of an eye, everything changed. I could never again imagine the blissful ignorance of living just for myself. Indeed, I had always thought that it was in marriage that we learned to give of ourselves and put another's needs before our own. Marriage was only the training ground. It was at our son's birth that I learned of something even greater, an emotion completely new and terrifying and sacred. It was only in light of my child that I began to understand—to aspire to—love of a sacrificial kind. The kind of love that God extended, through the suffering and death of his own Son, to us.

Unconditional, boundless, consummate love.

SUBMISSION

It was a day like many others days. There were diapers and dishes, books and blocks, meals and messes. Alexander and Emily were both under the age of three.

That evening, I was to receive a teaching award from my graduate department at UCLA. My professors and peers would all be there for the end-of-the-year celebration. Having dressed carefully in clothing not doused in spit-up, I waited for Daniel, who was late. I was getting nervous.

At last, he came, limping down the gangway.

"What happened?" I asked as he stepped inside the boat.

"I twisted my ankle."

"Oh, I'm sorry."

Daniel was quiet, unusually grim.

"The kids have had dinner," I assured him. "You'll just need to bathe them and get them ready for bed."

"I can't take care of the kids tonight!" he insisted. "I need to elevate and ice my ankle." As Athletic Director and P.E. teacher of a private French high school, Daniel was on his feet much of the time.

I was deeply incensed. After *all the nights* I had risen to tend to them, *all the days* I had spent taking care of their every need. Certainly the man who had fathered them could manage for a few short *hours*?

"I need to attend the award presentation," I bristled. Having kept up on my coursework, passed my doctoral exams, and fulfilled my duties as a teaching assistant while parenting first one and now two children, I had worked hard to stay on the rails. I longed to bask in the small accolade of my achievement.

"I won't be long—a few hours, depending on traffic."

Daniel gazed at me sharply, shook his head imperceptibly. I ignored the gesture.

Instead, I handed the kids sippy cups full of chocolate milk and hugged them all goodbye. Then, without contrition, I ran out the door.

"They'll be fine," I told myself while rushing to the car. "I'll be gone for three hours, max. Unless there's traffic....They'll be fine." As I revved the engine and pulled onto the street, I prayed for green lights and the Lord's covering.

Yet by the time I had reached the corner, I could no longer deny the pesky tinge of guilt. The Holy Spirit was relentless.

But God, it would look really unprofessional if I didn't show up.

Surely, the Lord would understand my desire to work as if unto Him.

What will they think of me if I don't even come to receive my award?

Pride. Pride. Pride. I hated recognizing it. Hated that I was unwilling to subdue it.

I never go to anything, God. I'm always with the kids.

Ugh. The whiny nature of my prayer was unmistakable.

Then a memory from the mothers' group I attended flashed through my mind. The weekly gatherings at our church had been a lifesaver for me, the first of my friends to have children. One recent guest speaker had been a model and actress. Though she had attended the group from time to time as a participant, she was there that day to promote her new cookbook.

Her hair was shiny, her outfit stylish. No baby fat hid behind burp towels, no baggage below her eyes betrayed sleepless nights. We—the more frumpy and haggard mothers assembled—looked with a mixture of admiration and envy upon this woman who evidently had it all. We smiled in rapt attention as she told us about her career. We *ooohed* and *aaahed* as she shared recipes learned in the kitchen of her Italian grandmother. We fantasized about future triumphs that might bring us such acclaim.

Following her presentation, we were invited to ask questions. How had she become a model? Was she still working in that field? Were there any new roles that she would be playing as an actress? We fawned sincerely, shamelessly.

One woman then asked if her children were proud of their famous mother. Our previously ebullient speaker became quiet, her eyes darkened. The room stilled as she weighed her words.

"I have four children," she began, her tone warm, soft. "The oldest, from my first marriage, were young when I was trying to make it as a model and actress. It's so competitive, so cutthroat," she insisted, shaking her head. "I was so worried about getting older, about missing my chance."

We nodded, empathetic.

"I wasn't around as much as I should've been," she confessed. "And they suffered for it." There was grief on her face, pain and regret in her voice. "The oldest has struggled with addiction; my second doesn't want to have much to do with me...."

There was a collective gasp. Then a painful silence engulfed the room.

I was taken aback by her candor. I think we all were. Hadn't we been told as women that we could have it all?

Our speaker resumed with a sigh, her voice brighter. "I've been blessed to be able to start over with a new family. I work less..."

She paused, reflecting.

"The thing is," she declared, finally finding the words, "the thing is: my girls *don't care* what I do for a living. They *don't care* that I'm famous. They're just happy to have me as 'Mom.'"

Waiting at the stoplight, a deep sense of conviction came over me. My life—as a Christian, by definition; as a wife and mother, by sacred trust—was no longer my own.

And I didn't want to have such regrets.

Okay, Lord. Okay.

The party would go on without me. The award was still mine. My family needed me then more than my classmates and professors did. I would not, I decided then and there, prioritize my professional pursuits over them.

They were my life's great work now.

Turning the car around, I went home.

WHAT ONLY GOD CAN DO

Wednesday morning moms' group was a blessing. Held at Bel Air Presbyterian Church in West Los Angeles, the gathering brought together some amazing women. There was a *Los Angeles Times* staff editor and the former actress-model-cookbook writer. There were even some stay-at-home moms, which, in Southern California in the year 2001, were nearly as unconventional as living on a boat. I always looked forward to the weekly congregation of like-minded women. I coveted the advice, encouragement, and commiseration of these sisters in Christ.

The program always began with a devotional and prayer time before a speaker with some knowledge of the subject matter would present riveting information on such eminent issues as potty training and sibling rivalry. I took notes. That morning, Laura served as moderator. Smiling over the room from behind the podium, the keen newspaperwoman's gaze finally brought the assembly to an anticipatory silence. Then, following a brief exhortation, Laura opened the floor for prayer requests.

"Today," she began haltingly, "today, I think we should pray for things that only God can do." Her tone was provocative, daring.

Ladies exchanged hushed whispers. Laura scanned the room, straightened her neck.

"That way," our emcee explained, "we can see that it was Him."

I raised my eyebrows. What an exciting proposition. Who wouldn't want to see God move?

The hall was still but for the sound of cooing infants. Ladies stirred in their seats. Laura waited.

I had been praying for months for a way for us to move back "home." I missed having family around and regretted having to spend the few resources we had on travel to see them. Then there was my mother, who lived alone and was now battling a horrible autoimmune disease. Dad, too, was aging. How wonderful it would be for the kids to have grandparents close by. I yearned, also, for the closer proximity of nature—the flora, fauna, fresh air, and clean water of the great Northwest.

But my educational goal—a Ph.D. in French—promised limited professional opportunities. Having just recently completed my doctoral exams, I nervously watched as colleagues with much better resumes than mine either moved to Nowheresville to work as a professor or took jobs in private high schools.

I had faith in a God who could move mountains. Was this a mountain that He would move?

I raised my hand.

"Yes?" Laura pointed to me.

"I've been going to school with the goal of being a French professor." My voice quaked nervously. "I would *really like* to be a French professor. But those jobs are few and far between and I want to be closer to my family and raise our kids in Small Town, America...." How selfish I sounded. I, I, I, want, want, want. Other needs were certainly more important.

But the Lord had been so good to me. And I believed in his desire to bless us.

"Plus, I would really like to work at a Christian institution." In graduate school, we were repeatedly warned against talking about anything related to faith. "It would be hard to teach in an environment hostile to Christianity." My laundry list was ridiculous. I knew it. Why not ask for a unicorn?

"So," I concluded intrepidly, "I would really like to work at either Whitworth or Gonzaga."

A buzz of ladies' conversation filled the chamber. Several women nodded in approval. Others offered affirmations of God's ability to bring it to pass. The ice broken, a few other mothers dared to make similarly bold requests. Finally, we bowed our heads and together offered our praise and petitions to the Holy One of Israel.

As I stood in line to pick up the kids, an unfamiliar face approached me.

"I was looking for you," she began, her expression friendly. "My dad used to be the Dean of Faculty at Whitworth."

"Well, that's a fun coincidence," I acknowledged. I had only recently become aware of the small, Christian university in Spokane, Washington in my search for potential future employers. Still, I was dubious about how a former employee of a far-away university could have any impact on the school's need for a French professor.

"I'll call him and see if he knows anything," she offered.

"Thanks," I nodded. "That's kind of you."

The following week, she brought me the email address and phone number of the new Dean of Faculty. With nothing to lose, I sent an email introducing myself and expressing my interest in the institution. Because I still needed to write my dissertation, I also mentioned our three to five-year timeline. I attached a link to my new online resume—more to show off my technological savvy than my credentials.

The very next day, I received a reply. "We appreciate your interest in Whitworth. A search is, in fact, currently underway for a French professor.

The position is half-time. I have passed your information along to the search committee. You should expect to hear from them shortly..."

My head was spinning. Whatever I had expected, it was not that.

The chair of the committee contacted me and we scheduled a phone interview. I also provided the names and contact information of several of my professors and teaching assistant supervisors.

The following day, I received an email from my dissertation director. He needed to see me pronto.

Evidently, the search committee had contacted him.

My heart raced as I approached Dr. C's second-floor office. For while this senior professor had always treated me with courtesy, he was the one who would ultimately sign off (or choose not to sign off) on my terminal degree. Then again, I had enjoyed few tête-à-tête interactions with Dr. C. Due to both my chronic sense of inadequacy inspired by brainy and ambitious peers and—more recently—the arrival of babies, I had spent as little time on campus as possible. Inhaling deeply, I knocked on the heavy wooden door.

"Come in!" a voice inside bellowed.

Seeing me enter, Dr. C spent no time on formalities.

"Did you know that Whitworth is a *Christian* university?" he barked.

I was taken aback. I had expected him to ask about my professional accomplishments so as to better promote my application. This line of questioning caught me off guard.

"Yes," I confessed, finally. "Yes, I did."

Clearly, my dissertation advisor was unaware of my beliefs. Like my two pregnancies, carefully hidden beneath books and oversized blazers, I had somehow managed to conceal this essential element of my person. The thought was unsettling. I was, after all, supposed to shine God's light in the world.

Obviously, I was not doing a very good job of it.

Dr. C stared at me quizzically, lifted his glasses to rub his eyes, and then stared at me again. The musty smell of books was pungent.

"It's also a good school," I advanced finally, interrupting the awkward silence.

Dr. C sat mutely, uncharacteristically quiet. I thanked him for any recommendation that he could provide and took my leave.

The phone interview with the search committee was somewhat challenging to manage with two toddlers on a boat. Though I had locked myself in our state room, the happy noise of children playing was impossible to mute. Remarkably, Alexander managed not to hurt his sister and Emily succeeded in not bawling out her brother during the 30-minute conference call. At the conclusion of the interview, the search committee even wanted to fly me to Spokane for an on-campus interview.

Within a few days, a program assistant emailed me the proposed itinerary for my visit. It entailed meetings with the search committee as well as the university's president, chaplain, and dean. I would teach a class, share one meal with students and another with the faculty committee. I was to give a campus-wide presentation, attend a chapel service, and even meet with a local realtor.

My stomach churned. The prospective schedule would require me to be gone for *three whole days.*

"I can't leave for that long!" I lamented to Daniel over dinner. Emily, buckled firmly in her hook-on high chair, tested the acoustics of the glass table with her spoon. Alexander, who had jumped from his seat to grab his current favorite Matchbox vehicle, was quickly admonished to stay at the table during meals. "What would we do with the kids?"

Daniel scratched his head pensively. "I'll see if I can get a day off..."

A day. But certainly not *three.*

The next morning, I phoned the chair of the committee and quickly cut to the chase.

"Does the interview really require me to stay *two* nights?" I knew that I sounded unprofessional. But what was the alternative? "We have young children and no childcare."

I held my breath as the chair of the Modern Languages Department mused silently on the other end of the line. Would this professional woman take a chance on a candidate who couldn't even manage the standard interview schedule?

"I'll talk to the committee," she offered, finally. "We'll see what we can do."

And, remarkably, to even that they agreed.

So it was that within two months of one audacious prayer, I received an offer of employment at Whitworth University.

It was crazy. Astonishing. Miraculous.

Something only God could do.

DECEPTION

Two-year-old Emily was "helping me" make dinner in the kitchen while four-year-old Alexander played quietly upstairs. A little too quietly, I decided.

"Alexander?" I called, climbing the half-flight of stairs to his room. "Alexander, what are you doing?"

Seeing me, Alexander jumped up and ran past me into the bathroom, quickly closing the door behind him.

The man and his wife heard the Lord God... So they hid from the Lord God among the trees. Then the Lord God called to the man, "Where are you?"[1]

"Jus' minit!" Alexander's speech was sloppy, muddied.

"Okay." I waited. Though I had moved nearer to the closed door of the lavatory, I perceived no typical bathroom noises. "Are you alright?"

"Hmm-hmm."

[Adam] replied, "I heard you walking in the garden, so I hid. I was afraid because I was naked."[2]

Something was amiss. I waited a few seconds more before tapping on the door and pushing it open.

Alexander stood, fully dressed, between the sink and the toilet. Brown juice dripped from the sides of his lips.

"What's in your mouth?!" I gasped.

He swallowed then, hard. Eyes darting around, he looked for a means of escape. I blocked the doorway.

"What were you eating?" I insisted.

The Lord God asked. "Have you eaten from the tree whose fruit I commanded you not to eat?"[3]

Alexander shuffled his feet, mumbled incomprehensively. Finally, he raised his eyes to meet mine.

"Nothing."

"Nothing?" I couldn't believe my ears. "Son, you had something in your mouth!"

Alexander cowered slightly, but repented not.

"No, I didn't."

My heart pounded in my chest.

Stepping closer to grab his little cheeks, I saw them: Tootsie Roll wrappers. Then leaning down to smell his breath, warm and sweet, I extracted the evidence from the trash.

"What are these?"

The Lord God asked..., "What have done?"[4]

"I dunno."

A sword pierced my heart.

Deception. Separation. Loss.

And thus, sin entered the world.

TREE OF LIFE[1]

Though trained in pedagogy and critical theory, practiced in verb conjugations and literary analysis, I was unprepared to oversee a university classroom that included a student with Asperger Syndrome. Isabella was my first. Enrolled in a third-year French composition course, Isabella qualified for educational accommodations intended to promote her success: she could ask to sit in the same location each session, schedule an extended amount of time to take an exam, request class notes from her peers.

The challenge was not her intellect. Isabella was bright; her written French, good. The difficulty was engaging this student aurally and orally in the conversational-style classroom that I endeavored to cultivate. For despite her lively efforts to talk with me, when it came to interacting with her classmates, Isabella remained aloof. During assigned pair and group work, she was quiet, disengaged. And while I circulated among the students, verifying their understanding, promoting conversation in groups that seemed uncommunicative, I struggled to hold Isabella's interest in the task at hand.

Isabella's classmates were remarkably gracious. They greeted her affably each day. They invited her to join them on small-group exercises. They waited patiently as she formulated replies in her second tongue.

I was thankful to be teaching at a Christian college.

The penultimate assignment for the course was to be an oral presentation. After weeks of in-class practice, students would chose a canonical poem for which they would prepare a textual analysis. Their fifteen minute exposé was to include a Powerpoint slideshow or other visual display intended to help the listeners follow along. At the end of the presentation, each presenter was expected to field questions from classmates and corrections from me. The final assignment, then, would be a revised and improved textual analysis in written form.

Isabella came to see me in my office.

"I don't think I can do it, Madam Schrambach!" Though sitting directly across from me at my desk, her eyes darted around the room nervously.

"What do you mean, Isabella?"

"Well," her leg bounced up and down incessantly, "I'm afraid the other students will laugh at me."

I pondered this for a moment. Never had I observed anyone in our class be anything but kind to Isabella. I wondered what her high school experience had been.

"No one's going to laugh at you, Isabella." I assured her.

"What if I mess up?" she blurted. "I'm not very good at talking in French. We didn't speak much in my high school class."

"That's why we practice," I reminded her. "We can't get better if we don't practice."

Isabella's eyes continued to flit this way and that.

"But my French isn't perfect."

"*No one's* French is perfect," I insisted. "They all make mistakes, too."

Isabella looked deflated.

"I'm sure you'll do great," I said by means of conclusion. "Let me know if you have questions."

My visitor heaved deeply and stomped out of my office.

Isabella's presentation day finally arrived. Students were visiting in low tones, slowly taking their seats when she burst into the classroom and made a beeline for me.

"I can't do this, Madam Schrambach. I just *can't.*"

Isabella's face was frantic. Perspiration dripped from her hairline.

The other students quieted to listen.

I mentally reviewed Isabella's options. The presentation was only worth five percent of the overall grade in the course. The feedback she received from our interaction, however, would help to improve her final paper, worth an additional ten percent of the semester total. Isabella's grade would take a big hit if she didn't do the presentation.

"You *can* do it, Isabella," I whispered firmly, wishing I could take her shoulders in my hands, lift their sagging demeanor. "I *know* you can do it."

By then, it was class time. With three presentations and questions to fit into the 55 minute session, I could do no more to prod and persuade.

"*Bonjour, tout le monde,*" I called out, signaling that instruction time had begun.

Students hushed and lent me their attention. Isabella fretted as she took her seat near the front. Her name figured first on the list of presenters that day.

"Isabella," I called. "Please come to the front to get set up."

Isabella looked at the table before her, shook her head.

"Isabella," I called a second time, gently but urgently. "It's time for your presentation."

The young woman remained in her seat.

The other students looked at each other, looked to me to see how I would proceed.

I waited only a few moments before making the decision to invite the second presenter to come forward. With some reluctance, he did, eyeing Isabella as he walked by her—perhaps hoping, as I did, that she might change her mind. She did not.

Isabella continued to stare at the table in front of her during the performances of one and then another classmate. Every now and again, she heaved an audible sigh. She took no notes and posed no questions.

The presentations finished, fifteen minutes of class time remained.

"Isabella," I offered, again, "this is your last chance. Please come forward to share your work."

It was there, in her hands. I could see it. She had done the analysis, typed up her report.

Isabella acted as if she had not heard me. Her eyes remained on the floor. Her knees bobbled incessantly.

"You should do it, Isabella," a neighboring student prompted her encouragingly.

"Yes, you should do it!" others joined in.

Isabella looked up for the first time since class had begun. She seemed surprised that her classmates would care about her or her presentation. Turning her head to look around the room, she took in the chorus of supporters.

Seeing Isabella's reaction, more students joined in the cheer.

"You can do it!"

"Come on, girl!"

"Go, Isabella!"

Isabella soaked in the revelry. Her reddened features softened into a small grin. Then, closing her eyes in what appeared to be an effort at concentration, she drew her hands into tight fists and burst from her seat.

"Okay, okay," she huffed. "I'll do it!"

"Yay!" her classmates cheered.

Isabella tromped to the front of the room. The other students exchanged sympathetic glances as she mumbled nervously to herself. Isabella loaded her slideshow onto the classroom computer and assured its appearance on the overhead projector. Then, looking up at the ceiling, she began.

With a flush in her cheeks, Isabella explicated her poem with precision and dexterity. After situating the author in his historical time period, she explicated the poem's rhyme and meter, assonance and alliteration, symbolism and overall significance. Isabella's visuals were clear; her imperfect French, bold and understandable.

At last, she turned to me to announce the presentation's conclusion.

"That's it."

"Bravo!" I smiled back warmly. "Bravo."

The classroom erupted. There were whistles, applause, and shouts of acclamation.

"Is-a-bel-la! Is-a-bel-la!"

Standing to their feet in ovation, Isabella's peers celebrated the achievement of their classmate.

Isabella beamed. Looked up. Looked down. Stood still to take it in.

She was no longer an outsider, but a friend.

"A GOOD DAY FOR ME"

"She's gone." My grandma's voice on the phone was weak, hoarse.

"Gone?" It was early, 6 a.m. I had jumped from bed to grab the phone from the kitchen and run outside so as to not wake the family.

"Your mother, dear. She's gone."

"No," I whispered, tears falling from my eyes. "*Noooo.*" I collapsed grievously onto the outdoor couch.

Mom had struggled for years with Dermatomyositis. Recently, in anticipation of her 40-year class reunion, she had decided to go off some of her medication—the steroids, in particular—so as to lose a few pounds. Consequently, she had become extremely weak. My grandmother had taken her to the hospital just the night before. I had planned on going to see her that day.

But I was too late. She was gone.

Mom had always been charming, vivacious, fun. Yet the previous five years had been difficult. The pain and the prescriptions had taken their toll. Stubborn, Mom didn't always follow the doctors' advice. Cautious with money, she had more than once opted for the generic version of a drug only to discover that it didn't mix well with the others. (Once, we found her crawling on the floor of her home, believing that she was in a jungle.) Intractable, Mom was unwilling to move to be closer to us as she felt responsible for her parents, who lived nearby.

Mom was only 57.

The horrible part was that I had considered on at least one occasion how it would've been easier if she passed.

I felt like it was my fault. The Lord must have read my evil thoughts and taken her. I was terribly, eternally mortified that I had ever allowed such an idea into my mind. I felt complicit, despicable, loathsome, guilty of her death.

To top it off—Mom did not know the Lord. And I did. And I hadn't managed to introduce her.

All this ran though my mind as I laid crumbled on our back deck.

What would I do without her?

"I'm so sorry, Grandma," I heaved, finally remembering the grieving mother on the other end of the line. "*I'm so sorry.*"

The three hour drive to my hometown was a blur. Wracked with guilt, teeming with regret, my mind reviewed everything I should've said, everything I should've done and not done.

I didn't know she was going to die, Lord. I should have seen that she needed help.

God, please forgive me for not having been a better witness.

Oh Lord, I pray that she reached out to You before she died. Please save her.

My great-uncle Don was at the funeral home when I arrived. Together, we went in to see her body. Laid out on what looked like a stretcher, her skin was cool and clammy, her lips a pale blue. Though I recognized the features, the shell that had housed her spirit was only a shadow, a poor counterfeit of my mother.

She was gone.

If I prayed in faith, I wondered, stretched out my body onto hers, would the Lord revive her as He had the widow's son when Elijah asked?[1]

Would Uncle Don think me mad? I regretted his presence with me.

We stood in the room for minutes, hours. We left her there in silence.

What would I do without her advice? What would I do without her kind words and encouragement?

For the first time in my life, I felt very, very alone.

I went to her home of 30 years, the house in which I had grown up. I wanted to get her address book so I could call her friends and other far-away relatives. I wanted to smell the familiar odor of her Shalimar perfume. I wanted to be where she had last been alive.

A small, white paper was taped to the writing desk next to the front door. Mom had been a neat person; this was out of place. I pulled it off gently. The note, which looked to have been a portion of a church bulletin, had been cut around a Bible verse: "I have fought the good fight, I have finished the race, I have kept the faith. -2 Timothy 4:7."

That was strange. Mom had never talked about faith. Though she had certainly believed in God, she had never submitted her life to God's lordship or made a personal confession of faith. While we were growing up, Mom had occasionally dropped my brother and me at the nearby Lutheran church for Sunday school. She, however, had never made it to the sanctuary. (It had never been clear to me whether this practice was intended to promote belief in us or to grant an hour of respite for her.) Since becoming a Christian, I had dragged Mom to church with us whenever we were in town. On such occasions, she would inevitably file her fingernails or clean out her purse during the sermon.

Maybe she just identified with the "fought the good fight," part, I thought. Or maybe she sensed that her "race" was coming to an end.

How sad to think that she might have known this and not shared it with anyone—not share it with me.

Wondering through the house, trying to take everything in, I looked for—hoped for—other signs of belief, a conversion of which I was ignorant. The only manifestation of Christianity I found was the book that I had given her a few months earlier: Rick Warren's *Purpose Driven Life*. While it rested on her night stand, no book mark revealed whether or not she had ever perused its pages. Alas.

My dad and I spent the next few hours calling family and friends. Having worked my way to "F" in her address book, I found a note that she had inscribed above the list of names: "FUNERAL SONG: 'Lord, I Hope this Day is Good' by Kris Kristofferson."

"Dad, I think Mom wanted this song at her funeral. Look! She wrote it in her address book."

Dad nodded wistfully. Though they had been divorced for some 25 years, they had remained cordial, even friendly as the years passed. In his own way, he, too, grieved her loss.

"Well, let's go get it for her."

We jumped into the car and headed to Rockin' Rudy's where the owner, a friend of Dad's, helped us look through Kris Kristofferson's albums. Nothing resembled the title that Mom had penned.

I shouldn't have been surprised. I remembered when she had thought that the words to the theme song from the film *Caddyshack* ("I'm alright, nobody worry about me...") were "Hamburger stand." (Really.) I smiled at the memory. Listening to yet another Kris Kristofferson song, I found it somehow fitting that her last ruse would be to send us on a wild goose chase.

Oh, how I would miss her.

Still, it felt so very important to follow her wishes. Since we could not bring her back to life, we could at least honor her in this funeral request.

Dad and I spent an hour listening to Kris Kristofferson's catalog of music. I finally chose a song that I deemed suitable for the service and we returned to his place. While Dad watched television, I worked on her obituary.

My eyes were puffy the next morning when I walked into the kitchen. On the counter was a note in Dad's hand: "2.02 Lord I Hope this Day is Good by Don Williams." The artist's name was underlined.

He had evidently solved the puzzle. Waiting for him to emerge from his bathroom, I started a pot of coffee.

"So how'd you figure it out?" I asked, holding up the paper.

"I'd fallen asleep," Dad began. He often slept in his chair in front of the television, which he left on all night. "I woke up to a show about country music. And there it was: Don Williams and that song!"

How crazy, I thought. What a strange coincidence. Though I had grown up with a steady diet of country music, I had never heard of the song—or Don Williams.

"What does '2.02' mean?"

"That was the time it came on TV: 2:02 a.m."

My jaw dropped. A tingle shot up my spine. Not only had Dad woken in the middle of the night to a twenty-year old song that my deceased mother had requested at her funeral, but he had done so almost 24 hours to the minute from the time of her passing. (The death certificate would indicate 2:20 a.m.) If that weren't enough, Dad got out of his chair, found a piece of paper and pen, and wrote down not just the song and artist, but *the time it came on TV.*

It felt like the twilight zone.

We were at the door of Rockin' Rudy's when it opened. In the car, on the way back to Dad's, we listened to the prayer that Don Williams had put to music:

Lord, I hope this day is good.
I'm feelin' empty and misunderstood.
I should be thankful, Lord, I know I should,
But Lord, I hope this day is good.

Lord, have you forgotten me?
I've been prayin' for you faithfully.
I'm not sayin' I'm a righteous man,
But Lord, I hope you understand.

I don't need fortune and I don't need fame.
Send down the thunder, Lord, send down
the rain.
But when you're plannin' just how it will be,
Plan a good day for me.

It was a sad song, a song of desperation. Hearing the lyrics, I understood—perhaps for the first time—the misery of Mom's painful existence, the sorrow of her aloneness.

And I again suffered the guilt of all that I had done and had not done.

The funeral was lovely—a beautiful celebration of a beautiful soul. As Providence would have it, the newly-ordained son of Mom's dear friend, Patsy, was in town and able to conduct the ceremony. My brother and I spoke tearfully (a gift that she had given us both) about our wonderful mother. Hundreds of friends came to honor her memory.

Back home, without the distraction of writing her obituary, composing her eulogy, planning her funeral, cleaning out her house, *doing something* to honor her, I was miserable. Wallowing in grief and despair, I wondered if I would ever be able to move on. Wondered if I would ever be able to forgive myself.

I was cleaning the house one Saturday morning when the doorbell rang.

"Hi, Bendi." Our neighbor Pam stood on our front steps with a card in her hand. I had always enjoyed my conversations with this kind woman and mother of a daughter about Emily's age.

"Hi, Pam!"

"Bendi, I just learned about your mom. I am *so sorry.*"

"Oh, thanks, Pam." I swallowed, tried to stifle the tears.

"She must've been young!"

"57."

"Ugh," Pam shook her head. "I'm *very* sorry." She lowered her eyes in sympathy. Still, my neighbor stood before me, card in hand. I could tell she wanted to say something.

"Did she know the Lord, Bendi?"

I hated that question. Hated it because I wasn't sure. Hated it because I doubted. Hated it because of all the things I had done and had not done.

"Oh, Pam," I confessed. "I don't know." Tears spilled from my eyes. Pam reached to embrace me and we hugged in the doorway.

Would I ever again be able to talk about her without weeping?

"Thank you," I said, finally, pulling away.

"Bendi," Pam looked at me earnestly, "I know this is going to sound strange, but I spent some time praying before choosing a sympathy message." Pam gestured at the envelope in her hand. "I didn't want to buy the wrong card, you know?"

I nodded.

"But, in the end," she continued, "I felt like the Lord told me that your mom *did* know Him." She smiled timidly and extended the missive to me.

"Thanks, Friend."

Oh Lord, I hope she's right!

Five years later, Mom's friend, Patsy, phoned. She was coming to Whitworth for a summer ministry conference and wondered if we might get together for lunch. I happily agreed.

Patsy and I caught up on our lives, our children, her grandchildren. We spoke of the faith that we shared. Talk turned to Mom and her premature death.

"You remind me so much of her, Bendi!"

"I miss her, Patsy. It was such a great loss."

"It was... and I miss her, too. " We sat together for a moment in silence.

"I have grieved for her so much, Patsy. I am so sad that she didn't know the Lord. I feel so responsible..."

"But Bendi," Patsy interrupted, touching my hand gently, "your mom *did* come to know the Lord at the end. "

I was stunned. Shocked. Dubious.

Could it really be true?

Was I as dense as Peter?

"Are you *sure*, Patsy?" I begged, emotion overwhelming me. "How do you *know*?"

"Oh, I *am* sure, Bendi," Patsy insisted, pulling me into a comforting embrace. "Before she died, your mother, she *told* me!"

FIREWORKS IN HEAVEN

It was the 4th of July and we had invited friends to spend the afternoon with us at our little cottage on the lake. It also happened to be a Sunday, and our church was nowhere near our cabin. So much needed to happen before our guests arrived. From the moment I woke up, I stressed about how it would all get done.

"Maybe we should skip church today," I suggested to Daniel. "I need to clean the cabin and make the salads and put the berries on the cake..."

"It'll be fine," he assured me. "We'll all help."

I allowed myself to be convinced. It was the right thing to do. Still, I was in serious taskmaster mode all the way to church.

"When we get to the cabin, I'm going to need everyone's help," I reminded Alexander and Emily.

"Yes, Mom."

"You guys need to pick up and..."

"Let's talk about it after church," Daniel injected.

"Okay," I sighed, biting my lip. "But just know," I turned to the kids, "that we need to leave right after the service. We won't be staying to play today."

"Yes, Mom."

The sermon washed over me like water on a duck's back. While the body of Christ worshiped, prayed, and received godly instruction, I checked the clock and made mental lists.

Daniel can thread the skewers. Emily can put the berries on the cake. Alexander can gather firewood...

The last song sung, I hurried us out of the sanctuary.

"You go get Alexander," I ordered. "I'll fetch Emily."

"Got it."

I rushed to the door of the auditorium and gave the volunteer our daughter's name. Minutes passed. Emily did not come.

"Can you call her again, please?" I asked the youth worker.

"Sure."

Daniel and Alexander joined me in the large entrance hall.

"I called her five minutes ago!"

"She's so social," Daniel remarked. "She's always the last one out."

"Yes, but I told her today that we needed to leave *right away*." My frustration was palpable.

"We'll go get the car," Daniel offered, "and meet you in front of the building."

"Thanks."

More time passed. I was finding it difficult to exchange pleasantries with familiar faces who greeted me.

"Can you please find my daughter, Emily?" I finally asked a youth leader.

"Of course," the young woman replied. "I'll be right back."

The clock indicated that church had now been out for 15 minutes. Parents were already starting to check in their kids for the next service. I was contemplating whether Emily's lack of consideration merited punishment.

At last, our daughter appeared at the door of the auditorium, the youth leader in tow. The joy on Emily's adorable face made it difficult be angry. Seeing me, she ran across the foyer, curls bouncing.

"Mom! Mom! Guess what?" Emily was breathless. Her whole body quivered with excitement.

"What, honey?" I kneeled to imitate her size.

"Mom, I just asked Jesus into my heart!"

The youth leader, now standing behind Emily, smiled and nodded. Our locked eyes misted with emotion.

"Oh, honey," I cried, gathering her in a bear hug, "that is *wonderful*."

Instantly, all the worries and preoccupations that had filled my mind just seconds before dissipated in the light of eternity.

Oh Lord, forgive me for prioritizing my desire to have things look good for friends over You.

Forgive me, God, for taking for granted the privilege of worshiping You with other believers.

Forgive me, Lord, for not expecting You to make an appearance...

"That is *so wonderful*, Dolly," I repeated, squeezing her little frame. "The best decision you'll make in your *whole life*."

CAUGHT ON TAPE

Cancer changed Dad. Not only did the calluses he had—weekly—cut off his feet with a razorblade soften (and disappear), the harshness and exactitude of his character softened. Dad softened. He held his tongue, for the most part, when helping dye Easter eggs with the kids—even when they were doing it "wrong." He sniveled with emotion when watching his favorite movie, *Miracle on 34 Street*.

He told us that he loved us.

We went to visit regularly. (I better understood Mom's sense of obligation to her own parents.) Dad and Darbi dog were always happy to see us.

"Who's that?" he pretended when the kids showed up in their Halloween costumes.

"Nice shot!" he raved when Alexander banked the eight ball in a game of pool.

"That's *neat*, honey," he cooed when Emily told him of her 20-point basketball game.

It was Sunday. We were finishing breakfast. It would soon be time to make our return trip home.

And Dad started coughing up blood.

Emergency room. Hospital admittance. Doctors. Tests. X-rays. When it was clear that Dad was not going to be able to leave the medical facility anytime soon, Daniel took the kids home.

And I called my brothers.

The doctors tried medicine, tubes, sedation. Nothing worked. They were unable to stop the bleeding. My bigger-than-life, eternal optimist father was weakening before my eyes.

"There's one last procedure we could attempt," the doctor explained. Though he spoke quietly, his manner was dire. "We could try to sew up his stomach."

Over the previous five years, Dad had lost significant portions of several internal organs in his fight against lung and esophageal cancer. His insides were a mess.

"If it doesn't work," the doctor continued, "there's nothing else we can do."

"Well, yes, let's try!" I agreed.

Of course, we would try! Why wouldn't we try?!

"Just to be clear, Miss. If we don't succeed, we would not revive him from the procedure." The doctor looked at me intently. "We would just make him comfortable until he passes."

My stomach twisted. My heart pounded. My mind raced.

I was not about to have the same regrets that had racked me after Mom's death. I knew what I had to do. I had to ask the absentee father with whom I had not lived since the age of five, the man that I had spent my childhood trying to please, the indomitable dad who told me, when I got teary, to go clean myself up, if he had professed Jesus as Lord.

Over the years, I had spoken to Dad about my faith. I had even narrated the story of Philip and the eunuch when explaining my decision to be baptized. Dad's name was Phillip; I had hoped that he might feel a kinship. Since my conversion, Dad had begun reciting prayers before meals, short speeches of thankfulness, at special family gatherings. I appreciated the gesture.

And yet, I did not know what decision Dad had made about the Cross.

I was not about to leave this question unanswered.

Dad was in pre-game mode. Dad was always in pre-game mode. His mantra was "PMA: Positive Mental Attitude." It had served him well over the years—and likely contributed much to his fight against cancer. He had already lived five years longer than the doctors had predicted.

Would PMA be enough this time?

"Dad," I began prayerfully. "I know you're going to be okay." I fought to hold back the tears. Emotions always made him nervous.

Dad squeezed my hand warmly. His eyes were clouded with pain.

"But Dad," I swallowed hard. "If you don't make it, will I get to be with you in Heaven?"

My father held my gaze steadily and nodded. "Yes."

A few days later, my brothers and I were making arrangements for the funeral. We looked at pictures, told stories, laughed at their funny Dad-impersonations. Within the grieving, it felt good to celebrate together the man who had blessed us with his love, positivity, humor, and can-do attitude.

"Hey, guys!" the youngest said. "I forgot to show you this!"

My brother took out his phone and began to look for something. Still in college, he was young to lose a parent. I was sorry for my half-brothers who, only in their early twenties, would have to take on the future without the advice and nagging, the encouragement and support of their earthly father.

"The other day—it was, I don't know, three weeks ago?—I called Dad and for some strange reason, I hit 'record' on my phone."

"That's awesome," another brother said. "Do you still have it?"

"I do." He set his cell phone on the table. "The weird part is, you can't hear me, only Dad. Here," he pushed start, "let's listen."

And there it was: the booming, boisterous sound of Dad—enthusiastic, vibrant, alive. The resonant voice that had announced hundreds of horse races and emceed dozens of fundraisers filled the room and quickened our hearts.

"I can hardly hear you!" Dad called.

"I was riding my bike," my brother whispered. The four of us were now huddled together around the table.

"Which test was that? " Dad resumed. "Oh, well *great*, honey. That is *great*. I'm *proud* of you!"

My eyed welled. How seldom I had heard those words. I knew that we had all craved them.

"Okay, Bud!" Dad cheered.

His tone was so warm, so expressive.

Why was it that we often didn't recognize what was most important in this life—faith, family, people, relationships—until faced with our mortality? I was thankful that Dad had discovered it.

"I knew *that*. Hahahaha!" Dad howled from the microphone. His cackle reverberated around us, pulling us in.

"Well, *honey*," Dad continued. "Number one, all you gotta do..."

"I was telling him about a test," my brother explained.

"That's part of your life!" Dad urged. "*Every day* the rest of your life is pumping yourself up."

PMA. It had become part of us all.

"And I *mean* that," Dad insisted. "I mean, I'd like to be in your back pocket every single morning the rest of your life. But I can't be."

Tears fell. We hung on every word. Dad's final pep-talk.

"But on the other hand, you can—in a way—put me in your pocket just by saying, 'Dad says that this is the first day of the rest of my life, and that's the way it's gonna be.' What happens is that, finally, you believe in yourself and you don't need to think about me."

How could we ever forget?

The gift of words, of laughter, of memories.

The gift of a life.

BENNY AND A BORDER COLLIE

Growing up, Dad always had a Labrador or two. Though they were all trained to be hunting dogs, they mostly slept at his feet in the living room. Krissy, the Chocolate Lab, had been gentle and motherly; Hannah, the Yellow Lab, vigilant and protective; Darbi, the Black Lab, smart and athletic. While I always enjoyed their company on walks in the park, the dogs were, for Alexander and Emily, among the best parts of visiting their grandpa.

With Dad gone and with him, the opportunity to play with his pets, Emily finally convinced us that we needed a pup of our own. Knowing nothing about dog breeds, I spent some time researching the different needs and personalities of the *canis lupus*: there were companion dogs and guard dogs, hunting dogs and herding dogs. It was overwhelming, really. I just wanted a dog who could swim and run and go for walks with us. So as to avoid accidents and the destruction of items by chewing—the latter, a characteristic of Hannah—I also wanted a dog that was intelligent. Less enthusiastic about the prospect of dirty paws and dog hair, Daniel wanted a dog that was *free*.

The ad on Craigslist seemed to fit the bill: "Free puppies! The mother is a Border Collie. All we know about the father is that he runs fast when caught in the heat of passion. The dad looked to be a yellow lab, however, as do the pups." We chose a golden one with white markings on her nose. We named her Daisy.

Border Collies, I learned, are extremely smart. Our Collie mix was no exception. With intensity and focus, Daisy learned hundreds of word and commands. Ears pricked attentively, she would pick up on even small variations of phrasing and pitch. She sought stimulation, mental challenge, work.

Fortunately, she had the kids to manage. Daisy served as permanent defender to Alexander's offense in the sport of the season—outside linebacker for football, defensive midfielder for soccer. A herder, she could tackle and bring down a child twice her size with her front legs. We quickly learned not to bring her sledding since she insisted on "rescuing" the children from their careening coasters, pulling them to safety with her teeth.

Daisy needed tons of exercise. It was great timing then that, when she was about a year old, Shelly invited me to train with her for a marathon. Daisy kept me company for many a mile. Though she initially ran on a leash, she quickly learned to stay right beside me. Trotting happily to my left, she would look up at me every so often, as if checking for my approval.

"Good, Daisy," I acknowledged. "Good girl."

It was around that time that I decided to attend a prophetic conference. The event was advertised as a gathering of worshipers and Christian leaders from around the country who would share what they believed was a divinely inspired word from the Lord. Following worship and a pastor-led prayer, the evening's guest speaker was introduced. The man, known as a Christian prophet, preached a short sermon, a message that he sensed was intended for that particular church. Unfamiliar with the man—or even services deemed "prophetic," my theological antennae remained on alert; I would not be deceived by false doctrine. Yet the exhortation was sound and the teaching, biblical. No one tried to handle snakes or walk through fire.

Following the address, the man invited the worship team back onto the stage. As we sang a hymn of response, the prophet circled slowly on the platform. He looked to be praying.

At the conclusion of the song, the worship leader asked the congregation to be seated. The lights in the sanctuary brightened. The band remained on the stage, playing softly. (I thought of Elisha's use of the harpist in 2 Kings, Chapter 3.)

The prophet returned to the center of the platform. "Oh Lord," he prayed, eyes lowered, "edify your church."

The prophet then scanned the congregation intently, as if looking for a friend who was saving him a seat.

"You, there," the man finally said, pointing to a couple on the right side of the sanctuary. "Please stand."

It took a few seconds for the young couple to be correctly identified. At last, hand in hand, they stood to their feet.

"The Lord wants you to know that He sees you," the prophet began, extending his right hand toward them in blessing. "The Lord sees your faithfulness."

The couple bowed their heads. The husband put his arm gently around his wife.

"You've been going through a difficult time, but the Lord is with you," the prophet continued. "He sees you, sees your good works. He is strengthening you in this season."

The husband nodded, taking it in. The wife wiped a tear from her cheek.

"A new day is coming!" the prophet's voice rose in conclusion. "A new day is here!" The congregation clapped in affirmation and the couple returned to their seats.

The service continued like that—the prophet would pick out someone from the audience and speak a word of encouragement or blessing to them before moving to another person. One young man was spurred in his gift of evangelism; one woman, praised in her ministry to other women. Every so often, the prophet would pause to request a small chorus or hymn. There was no one theme, no apparent order of those selected. Old and young, male and female, he addressed them all.

At one point, the prophet put his hand to his temple and closed his eyes. People shifted in their seats restlessly, expectantly.

"There's a name in my head that I can't quite make out," he said at last.

This was a new approach. I wondered at how close one must be to God to *hear his voice*, to make out a particular *name*.

That would be amazing, I thought, reflecting for the hundredth time on the inspiring faith of Jay and Joan.

"The Lord has a word for someone with a name that I can't quite make out," the prophet repeated. Then, opening his eyes, he uttered what he thought might be the name.

"Benny?"

My heart quickened hearing a name so like my own. I looked around to see who would receive the message. No one stood.

"Benji?" the prophet tried again, scanning the room with expectation.

Heat rose to my face. *Was it me? Was he trying to say something to me?!* Still, incredulous, I stayed in my seat.

"Well," the prophet sounded disappointed. "If you know someone by that name, I feel like the Lord has a message for someone with a name like that. Benny or Benji or..."

This was crazy.

Then a man two rows in front of me rose to his feet. I felt relieved. And disappointed. And mad at myself for not daring to stand.

"There you are," the prophet smiled at the man. "What's your name?"

"George."

"George?"

"Sometimes people call me 'Ben.'"

"Okay," the prophet nodded slowly, considering. "Okay! Well! George—Ben—I believe that I have a message from the Lord."

The prophet paused for a moment, weighing his words.

"Have you ever had a Border Collie?" he began.

This was ridiculous.

"No," George replied.

"I had a Border Collie growing up," the prophet mused, grinning at the memory. He sauntered back and forth as he spoke. "An amazing dog—so smart, so energetic. Wherever I was, if I called to him, he'd come running. He could hear my voice from miles around, it seemed. It was like he was always listening for me."

George, directly in front of me, stayed on his feet. Though I could not have seen his expression from my vantage point, I was not looking at him. With rapt attention, I focused on the words of the man on stage.

The prophet turned to face George—and me, right behind him.

"I believe that the Lord would say to you: keep listening to his voice—like my Border Collie did to mine. Fix your eyes, your ears, on Him. Train your ears to hear...to recognize...His voice."

Though the service continued, I don't remember anything that the prophet said after that moment or even how the ceremony ended. With single-minded determination, I vowed to hold onto that word, that message, that aspiration.

A good one for any George, Ben, or Bendi.

THE TELOS

Another Faculty Development Day—a time each semester when Whitworth classes were cancelled so that professors could receive instruction. This particular day featured a renowned guest speaker: Dr. S, a philosophy Ph.D. from a different Christian college.

I knew nothing about the prolific author who was introduced to us that Friday. Truth be told, I was barely keeping my head above water most weeks. My attention was focused mostly on what I had to do next.

Our days were packed to the gills, scheduled to the minute. Between my work, the kids' school, their sports and activities, domestic chores, and an occasional social event, my plate was full. Trying to be a good wife, a good mom, a good professor, a decent friend, and a generally healthy person, this was not an undertaking for the faint of heart.

Alexander and Emily were now in middle school at a rigorous charter academy. I was up late with them nearly every night—memorizing Greek and Latin roots, proofreading essays, helping with math. I had developed an eye twitch, which I was convinced was the result of one teacher's seeming persecution of Alexander.

"You are a waste of a front seat," she had told him. Evidently, she didn't appreciate our son's habit of gazing out the window during her instruction.

A day for me to sit and soak in information instead of doling it out was a welcome change of pace. I looked forward to what the bearded man before us had to say.

"Should a biology course—or an English course, or a calculus course— at a Christian college differ from its equivalent at a secular institution?" Dr. S posed rhetorically.

There was a murmur of discussion. Many of my colleagues nodded their assent.

"If, then, we believe that courses at a Christian institution *should* differ from their secular counterparts, *how* should they differ? In *what* should they differ?"

A respected physics professor raised his hand emphatically and spoke up before Dr. S could acknowledge him.

"All physics students must learn the fundamental principles of the discipline. There is no time in Physics 101 to incorporate matters of *faith*." He spoke forcefully, insistently, convinced of the rightness of his assertion. Turning to those seated around him, he looked for signs of their agreement. From my table across the room, I could not discern if he found any.

Dr. S remained unruffled. While he had planned on delivering a lecture, he was practiced in the art of reining in unruly pupils.

"Let's take a step back, then," Dr. S resumed. Pondering his next tack, he looked at his notes, stroked his beard. Then stepping out from behind the podium, he looked up, closed his eyes, and recommenced.

"The Greeks speak of the 'telos'—the end, purpose, or goal. Indeed, Aristotle's epistemology is based on an object's telos or inherent purpose, use, or aim. The telos of an apple tree, for example, is to grow and provide shade and, eventually, produce fruit for consumption; the telos of a shoe is to protect a foot." He opened his eyes to look at the physics professor and then around the room. "As Christians, we believe that the telos is God." He spoke slowly, deliberately, allowing us to consider and reflect. "He is the Alpha and the Omega, the beginning and the end. And while He created humans to be in relationship with Him, *He* is the ultimate goal or purpose, the final reason or end."

A shiver ran down my spine.

Dr. S continued his discourse, pacing leisurely back and forth in front of a large projection screen. He said many other wise things, all thoughtfully reasoned and compellingly presented.

I never got past the Telos.

What had I been doing? I asked myself in disgust.

"Do your homework!"

"Get ready for basketball/tennis/choir!"

"Have you memorized the poem yet?"

"What grade did you get on the test?"

"Have you practiced your free throws?"

"You should really take the advanced class, it will improve your SAT score."

"Don't forget to pack for this weekend's soccer tournament! We'll leave right after school."

Yes, we attended church most every week. Yes, we prayed before dinner and at bedtime. I always signed the kids up for a Christian summer camp and tried during the academic year to get them into a Christian small group with their classmates.

And yet, how much time did we spend each day—each week—pursuing the things of God? Serving, worshiping, memorizing Scripture? Not enough. Alexander and Emily knew more Latin prefixes than Bible verses!

I had not prioritized the most important thing. Indeed, I wasn't even sure if I had explicitly *told* them what the most important thing *was*. On the contrary, my words, my actions, even our weekly schedule reflected the world's priorities. Grades, test scores, athletic and musical achievements—though all good and of value—had become our gods. They had distracted us from the meaning of it all.

Jesus. It was all about Jesus.

Things at our house were going to have to change.

PLANNING FUNERALS

We had endured a season of significant loss. My mother, grandmother, grandfather, father, and sister-in-law all passed within the span of a few years. It had been a difficult time, one that I did not manage well. Preoccupied with death, an obsession that I began to judge—as Solomon[1]—as profitable, I talked about it *a lot*. Having planned the memorial services of several loved ones, I decided to communicate my own funeral wishes to our children—from the songs to the Scripture reading. I had decided on Psalm 139:1-18.

> You have searched me, Lord, and you know me. You know when I sit and when I rise; you perceive my thoughts from afar. You discern my going out and my lying down; you are familiar with all my ways. Before a word is on my tongue you, Lord, know it completely. You hem me in behind and before, and you lay your hand upon me. Such knowledge is too wonderful for me, too lofty for me to attain. Where can I go from your Spirit? Where can I flee from your presence? If I go up to the heavens, you are there; if I make my bed in the depths, you are there. If I rise on the wings of the dawn, if I settle on the far side of the sea,

even there your hand will guide me, your right hand will hold me fast. If I say, "Surely the darkness will hide me and the light become night around me," even the darkness will not be dark to you; the night will shine like the day, for darkness is as light to you. For you created my inmost being; you knit me together in my mother's womb. I praise you because I am fearfully and wonderfully made; your works are wonderful, I know that full well. My frame was not hidden from you when I was made in the secret place, when I was woven together in the depths of the earth. Your eyes saw my unformed body; all the days ordained for me were written in your book before one of them came to be. How precious to me are your thoughts, God! How vast is the sum of them! Were I to count them, they would outnumber the grains of sand—when I awake, I am still with you.

It was not surprising, then, that our guileless and gregarious daughter, who had by then attended a dozen such ceremonies, would share this information with others. The setting: her freshmen high school theology course.

"Good morning, class. Please take your seats!"

Young and handsome, Mr. Ptolemy was everyone's favorite. In his second year at the Jesuit high school (chosen for Emily, in part, because of the Telos[2]), Mr. Ptolemy brought creativity and care to the task of teaching the faith.

"Instead of a Catholic prayer this morning, does someone have a Bible passage that they would like to suggest?"

Always quick to show her precocious knowledge, Emily raised her hand.

"Emily?"

"We could read the Scripture my mom wants at her funeral!"

"Oh, goodness," Mr. Ptolemy frowned. "Is your mother, ill?"

"No, no," Emily reassured him. "My mom...she just likes to plan things."

The teacher nodded gravely. "I see." He hesitated, perhaps reconsidering his original offer, then relented. "And what passage is it?"

"Psalm 129," Emily replied confidently.

"Psalm 129," Mr. Ptolemy repeated, flipping to it in his Bible. "The Word of the Lord," he began with solemnity.

"'They have greatly oppressed me from my youth,' let Israel say; 'they have greatly oppressed me from my youth, but they have not gained the victory over me.'"

Mr. Ptolemy paused. Squinting at the text, he reviewed the number identifying the Psalm to ensure that he was reading the correct canticle. He was. Mr. Ptolemy then glanced up at our daughter, now shrunk down in her seat. Having only known her for a few weeks, he was uncertain what to make of this antic. He shook his head slightly in disappointment.

The other students eyed the new girl with curiosity.

Emily was mortified. It was the wrong passage, she knew, but not having the verses highlighted in her Bible like her mother did, she could not immediately rectify her error.

It was with reluctance that Mr. Ptolemy continued.

"Plowmen have plowed my back and made their furrows long. But the Lord is righteous; he has cut me free from the cords of the wicked..."

Mr. Ptolemy read to the bitter end of Psalm 129, which seemed, to Emily, an eternity. He closed his Bible carefully. The room was silent but for the sound of Emily's heartbeat pounding in her ears.

"Well," Mr. Ptolemy said finally, "that is going to be some funeral!"

NOËL

Fresh snow covered the earth that early December morning. Still, we had left home with plenty of time to arrive on campus for my 8 a.m. class. It was when dropping Emily at high school around 7:30 a.m. that catastrophe struck. The force of slamming the trunk of my little car caused some part of the chassis to fall to the ground. When I put the engine into first gear, there was resistance to my normal acceleration. Hearing the scraping of metal on icy cement, I turned back toward the curb, illuminated the hazard lights, and exited the vehicle.

It was not easy to look under the low clearance of my coupe in snow while wearing a dress and high heels. Both for Emily's reputation and to maintain a remnant of personal dignity, I prayed that I would not slip and fall as I circled the automobile to identify the problem.

Fortunately, a security guard recognized me as a woman in distress and approached.

"It's the skid plate," he determined, as if it were his left hand.

"The skid plate," I repeated blankly. I had never heard of it.

"Did you have an oil change recently?"

"Yesterday," I replied, still uncertain of the correlation. "So what do I do?" I would've called Daniel, but he was 45 minutes away, and this was urgent.

"Well, you need to have someone screw the skid plate back on."

"Can you do that?"

The security guard looked around to see if he were on Candid Camera. "No, ma'am," he replied finally. His tone was respectful, directive. "You'll need to go to a mechanic. There's one just a mile or so up the road."

I thanked him and was off. Noisily. Making a few sparks where the snow had melted. I would have been embarrassed if I hadn't been so worried about being late.

En route, I called our departmental program assistant.

"Hi Rachelle. It's Bendi."

"Hi, Bendi."

"Hey, I'm having some mechanical issues and I think that I might be a little late to my 8 a.m. class. It's in Room 125, just downstairs. Could I ask you to give them a little work to do until I get there?"

"Sure. What should I tell them?"

At the service station, I begged the nearest mechanic to reattach my now-damaged skid plate *immediately*. The middle-aged man with worn hands and a soft expression kindly obliged. Though I offered—with sincerity and persistence—he refused payment for his services. I vowed to return with Christmas cookies.

Arriving finally to campus around ten after eight, I rushed as quickly as I could—through snow wearing a dress and high heels—to the building where my class met. The grounds—void of students who were, at that hour, either in bed or in class—seemed ethereally quiet. It was as if the powdery white blanket had lulled all of creation into a serene slumber.

There would be no coffee for the students that day, a habit that I had practiced that academic term in an effort to extend hospitality to these early risers. I thought of the dear souls waiting for me in the classroom, all juniors and seniors who had chosen to take the introduction to French Linguistics course to satisfy the requirements for a major or minor in French. Among the group, there was a musician, an aspiring theologian, and a future librarian. There was a French and Spanish double-major intent on working as an interpreter, and two Political Science and French double-majors with plans for law school. An exceptional bunch, they had challenged and inspired me all semester. They were a group that would be missed.

My phone now indicated that it was 8:15 a.m., the time after which, by rule, students were excused to leave if a professor were not present. I wondered if they were even now gathering their belongings. Would I make them return to the classroom if I intercepted them as they made their escape?

Turning into the hallway of Room 125, I heard music, the sublime resonance of human voices harmonizing as one. Perhaps a professor in the neighboring classroom was showing a movie. This struck me as unusual, however, since I had thought that we were the only ones in this area of the building at this time of the morning.

Stopping to catch my breath just outside the closed door, I realized that the noise was coming from inside *my* classroom. I mentally reviewed what I had asked Rachelle to assign. Listening to music was not on the list.

Slowly, quietly, I opened the door.

My first thought was that I must be dreaming. This would explain the angelic chorus. My students, still unaware of my presence since gazing at their cell phones, were lifting up their voices together in song. For having finished the tasks that Rachelle had given them, they had decided to pass the time waiting for their professor by singing Christmas carols—in French.

A wee glimpse of Heaven.[1]

VOCATIONS

Emily had always been troubled by injustice. Even before the recent complaints about her curfew—earlier than that of most of her friends—she had agonized over events that she perceived as wrong, unjust, "not fair."

Our daughter was also wonderfully inquisitive, blessedly bright. It was a combination that resulted in some interesting obsessions. Emily read books about serial killers, school shooters, and the rape cases associated with one university's football team. She watched a documentary about the OJ Simpson trial and an investigative report theorizing that Kurt Cobain, deceased lead singer of the rock band Nirvana, had not committed suicide as reported but had been murdered. Most recently, for one school presentation, she had elucidated her class on the falsely-accused Duke lacrosse team.

"Is there anything we need to talk about, Dolly?" I had asked once, in partial jest. "Should we get you into therapy?"

But no. Emily judged these fetishes as completely normal.

"Who wouldn't be interested in law and order? Who wouldn't want to uncover the truth?"

When Emily had announced her plans for law school, however, I had mixed emotions: pride in her intellect and aspirations, misgivings about the implications of that choice for her and her future family. While I recognized the gifts that the Lord had given her and even the seeming burden for justice that she carried, I also knew that family life would be difficult to reconcile with success as a lawyer.

It was true that Emily might change her mind a hundred times—or at least a dozen. I had changed my major at least three times in college and then ended up pursuing graduate degrees in a totally different field. I had also been nearly certain that Alexander was going to become a fireman, so fixated had he been on fire trucks and fire engines (there is a difference) at the tender age of three. Our son's current passion for music, which began at age ten, seemed to have stuck.

I wondered for the hundredth time why the Lord hadn't simply affixed a unique instruction guide to each child upon their birth. It was such a grand responsibility to be a parent. The influence, though not consummate, was vast and weighty. This had not seemed problematic when they were preschoolers and I had promoted play dates with some classmates but not others. I hadn't thought twice about enrolling them in soccer and piano but not softball and orchestra. I had even cut their hair myself—without much mind to their preferences—until they were in middle school.

Emily was fifteen now, nearly sixteen, and Alexander seventeen going on eighteen. My advice was not as revered as it had once been. I recognized that my opinions would certainly not be the final word on their future vocational choices. Still, my words would probably figure in their deliberations—for better or for worse. My viewpoint might even promote or deter them from certain pursuits.

Speaking into their lives was a holy responsibility that I did not take lightly.

On the matter of law school, then, I had—for a while now—been responding positively though unenthusiastically to Emily's mention of it, all the while continuing to suggest other directions for her aptitudes. A conversation that I had at work changed all that.

It was the beginning of a new semester. With pomp and circumstance, the campus community was to gather for the biannual convocation ceremony. There, we would "celebrate the beginning of the semester, recognize important community members, and ask for God's blessings" on the year.

Faculty, clad in colorful academic regalia, had assembled in an adjacent building to await the bagpipe players who would lead us into the field house. Joining the large group already present, I looked for a friendly face with whom to exchange pleasantries and spotted Ingrid. A beloved German instructor, Ingrid was also a devoted mother of four remarkable children. Over the years, I had taken notice of her prayerful and wise oversight of their transition from home-school to high school to college and adulthood. I always appreciated her acumen and experience in shepherding those whom the Lord had entrusted to her.

Ingrid and I spoke briefly about departmental concerns and our courses that semester before moving on to the subject of our families. Ingrid's youngest, a year older than Emily, was in the midst of college application season. My colleague spoke of her daughter's choice of schools, the process, the excitement, the cost!

I told Ingrid about Emily and my upcoming trip to visit some universities, our daughter's interest in law school, and my reluctance to encourage it.

"But why, Bendi?"

"Oh," I hemmed, "I know that Emily wants to have a family—wants to be a big part of *raising* her family. What I *don't* know are any successful lawyers who work less than sixty hours a week."

Ingrid sighed. The growing chatter of faculty colleagues echoed throughout the gymnasium.

"Bendi," Ingrid mused carefully. "I want to tell you about my oldest."

The rising volume required us to draw closer together. Ingrid leaned to speak into my ear.

"Like Emily, our daughter always knew what she wanted to be. For her, it was medicine. She played doctor from time she was a little girl!" Ingrid paused to savor the memory, a grin spread across her lips. "But then, somehow along the way, she reasoned herself out of it—or someone else did—because she also wants a family."

I nodded, grateful once again for the academic schedule that allowed me time off with the kids each summer. Indeed, the Lord had worked out the details of my professional journey just perfectly. Better than I ever could have.

My colleague continued. "Our daughter is 25 now. Still single. She just returned to school to pursue her childhood dream."

"Good for her!" I cheered above the din of voices.

Ingrid leaned in again, her tone thoughtful.

"You never know what the future holds, Bendi. When they will marry... *if* they will marry...even *if or when* the Lord will bless them with children."

"That's true," I granted, still not fully convinced.

Ingrid's wise gaze held mine. She placed her hand gently on my arm as she uttered one final intuition.

"The Lord obviously created this passion in your daughter, Bendi. He must've done so for a reason."

I gasped, the air in my lungs temporarily suspended.

She was right.

Emily's interest in law school had nothing to do with us. Daniel and I had done nothing to promote our daughter's longstanding preoccupations. We hadn't introduced those subjects or read those books or even watched those shows with her. And unlike me at 17, Emily was not seeking the admiration of an inaccessible father.

God had put this inside of our daughter. He had even given her the brains to be successful at the academic challenge of law.

Who was I to discourage it?

So this is what it looked like to entrust my child to God. I was going to have to take my hands off the wheel.

What ever would I do with my well-used backseat driver's license?

FAITH-FILLED PRAYER

Darlene and I had met in college. Hers had been one of the friendly faces I had encountered at the Wednesday evening services on campus. Darlene had also been the one—the only one—to invite me, a near-stranger, to spend Thanksgiving of my freshman year with her and her family. Meeting Darlene for the first time, Daniel had designated her a big heart with little legs. At all of 5'2," it was an apt description.

Darlene was the first person I ever met who wrote Bible passages on notes for me. There had been this one:

> For this reason, ever since I heard about your faith in the Lord Jesus and your love for all God's people, I have not stopped giving thanks for you, remembering you in my prayers. I keep asking that the God of our Lord Jesus Christ, the glorious Father, may give you the Spirit of wisdom and revelation, so that you may know him better. I pray that the eyes of your heart may be enlightened in order that you may know the hope to which he has called you, the riches of his glorious inheritance in his holy people, and his incomparably great power for us who believe.[1]

She had also penned this, from Paul's letter to the church at Philippi:

> I thank my God every time I remember you. In all my prayers for all of you, I always pray with joy because of your partnership in the gospel from the first day until now, being confident of this, that he who began a good work in you will carry it on to completion until the day of Christ Jesus.[2]

And Darlene had sent me this one before finals' week that first semester of our freshmen year:

> Rejoice in the Lord always. I will say it again: Rejoice! Let your gentleness be evident to all. The Lord is near. Do not be anxious about anything, but in every situation, by prayer and petition, with thanksgiving, present your requests to God. And the peace of God, which transcends all understanding, will guard your hearts and your minds in Christ Jesus.[3]

The notes had marked me. Reading the Word of God in a handwritten missive brought it to life. It was almost as if the Lord had written it to *me*.

In college, Darlene and I had made a practice of walking on the beach and praying aloud together. We would stride and supplicate for an hour, traveling four miles on foot and infinite expanses in the spiritual realm. Twenty years later, we were still close—despite significant distance. We even continued to pray together on the phone.

It was a Thursday afternoon when Darlene called while her youngest children were occupied with a play date at her home. With little ones still underfoot, it was always best when my friend initiated our communication. We caught up as best we could on our families—news about our teenagers, the various developmental stages of her younger children, updates on our husbands, other miscellany.

"So how can I be praying for you?" Darlene probed.

"The kids, of course...my ladies' Bible study...," I paused to reflect. "You know, Dar, I always feel like I grow so much from these studies, from spending time in God's Word."

"Yeah...." She waited.

"Well, I wish that I could do more of these kind of things with Daniel. We go to church, he listens, but..."

"It would be nice to be growing together in the Word."

"Yes," I confirmed. "It would."

We both sighed.

I prayed first for my friend—for strength and wisdom and grace, for time and energy and provision, for health and mercy and covering for her, her husband, and their beautiful family.

Then it was Darlene's turn to pray.

"Thank you for Jesus, for coming to show us your love. Thank you for saving us, Lord, and blessing us with our families. Thank you for this friendship and for the privilege of coming to You in prayer."

From my location more than a thousand miles away, I joined my spiritual sister in praise and intercession.

"We lift up our children, God, and pray for your protection of them. We pray, too, for wisdom to parent them well. Help them to grow up in you, Lord."

"Yes, Father," I affirmed.

"For our husbands: please bless them with your favor. Help us to be good helpmates to them, to love and serve them well."

"Yes, Lord," I whispered.

"And for Daniel, God, please put a desire in his heart to be in your Word, to learn more about You. Draw him to it like a deer pants for the water and bless him for the time he spends with You."

"Thank you, God."

"Bless Bendi and the ladies in her Bible study. Knit them together in your love."

"Yes, Lord."

"Thank you, God, for your faithfulness to us, for your promises, and for your provision. We love you, Lord. In Jesus' name, Amen."

"Amen." I concluded. "Thank you, Friend."

By then Darlene's children were in need of attention. We said our goodbyes and hung up the phone.

Saturday evening, Daniel and I were sitting on our back deck enjoying the late summer colors. The tall grass on the hillside swayed in the breeze. While I flipped through the local paper, Daniel skimmed news articles on his phone.

"You know, I don't read much," my husband began. "But I've been thinking—I'd like to have a Bible verse sent to my phone every day. It'd be good to be reading a little of that. Could you help me get it set up?"

"Sure, Honey." I grinned. "I'd love to."

IRON SHARPENS IRON[1]

"Y̶ou and Kenna should do a Bible study together!"

It was a Saturday morning and Kenna was on her way over. I sat on the floor of Emily's room, coffee in hand. My 17-year-old daughter was laying on her bed, a post-shower towel wrapped around her. She was scrolling through her phone.

Drawing no reply, I persisted. "Or you could choose a Christian book to read and then get together to discuss it."

Emily eyed me, aloof. I was annoying her, I knew it. I didn't mean to. I was simply trying to help her take on her faith, dig in. Already, high school had not been easy.

The girls had been friends ever since Emily had complimented Kenna on her sparkly pink Toms in sixth grade. A kind, smart young woman, beautiful inside and out, Kenna's was an alliance worth promoting. And yet, while they had participated in several "tween" Bible studies together (organized by Kenna's supermom, Krista), they didn't talk about their faith and its implications for their lives—at least, not while I was in earshot.

On the occasion of their last hangout before beginning high school at different institutions, I had made the suggestion to Emily that they pray together—pray for each other and their next chapter.

"That would be weird, Mom."

"Would it?"

"Yeah."

Three years later, little had changed with regard to Emily's response to my propositions. I took my last sip of coffee and exited her room.

Kenna arrived—spirited and sparkling and sightly. We visited for a few minutes before she and Emily excused themselves. They found their way to our daughter's room, christened "Narnia" by Alexander several years prior due to its mystic ability to make Emily disappear for hours on end. The door clicked shut and they were gone.

That evening, I was preparing dinner when Emily came into the kitchen.

"Kenna and I talked about reading something together."

"That's wonderful," I replied, gratified that she had heard me. "So, what are you thinking?"

"Well, Kenna mentioned that it would be good to know more about Satan."

I stopped cutting vegetables and looked up to focus on my daughter's words.

"She knows a book that talks about Satan, so we can, like, know what he's thinking."

I set down the knife and shot up a silent prayer for wisdom.

"Don't you think it'd be better to know what *God* thinks about something than what *Satan* thinks about it?"

Emily's feelings were hurt. She had taken initiative and I had rejected it.

"Well, *Kenna and I* think it's a good idea." She turned to leave the kitchen. I cringed.

"Could we talk more about it?" I yelled from behind the counter. "Could you at least find out the name of the book?"

The sound of Emily's door closing was my only reply.

"Mom!" Emily was smiling as she came into my bathroom the next morning, the crease of her bed sheets still marking her rosy cheek.

"Good morning, Dolly," I leaned in to give her a hug.

"Good morning, Mom," she reciprocated with a squeeze.

"How'd you sleep?"

"Oh, fine, but Daisy makes a lot of noise. It's like she has sleep apnea!"

I laughed. Our aging Collie did make a lot of noise. Daisy seemed to stay close to the person that she felt most needed her "protection." Emily was evidently the weakest link these days.

"So, I was talking with Kenna on the phone last night."

"Mmm." I had turned back to the mirror to continue primping. Emily's reflection flickered in the glass.

"We talked about the book on Satan."

I ceased my grooming.

"And?"

"You know what book it is?" Emily asked, her voice teasing.

"What?"

"*The Screwtape Letters* by C.S. Lewis."

"That's funny," I grinned.

Emily nodded.

"It's a great book," I affirmed, returning to my makeup. "I read it in college. It really helped me to see the many ways the Enemy tries to tempt and disrupt us in our walk."

"Mmm." Her face glowed with vindication.

"I'll buy it for you."

"Great."

Emily's days that summer were filled with friends, part-time jobs, the college search. Early applications would be due in October. Our daughter finally settled on her list of schools, which included institutions both Christian and secular. Mine was not among them. Not only had she spent too many days—when sick or when her school was out of session and mine was not—in my office on campus or at the back of my classrooms to feel like Whitworth was anything but déjà vu, Emily wanted to see the world, live in other states. She wanted to fly. While our daughter would probably be accepted to most of the colleges where she applied, the final decision would likely come down to money.

School recommenced with a vengeance. Homework, soccer, volunteer hours, a university French class, Young Life, and many social events filled her weeks. As she began submitting college applications, we prayed that the Lord would make her next move clear.

And He did! Emily received a huge scholarship to her number one choice. And it was a Christian school! We celebrated the Lord's kindness and provision.

And I simultaneously grieved the impending "loss" of our daughter to a state far, far away.

Just before graduation, Emily received her roommate assignment: Keylynn, from California. We immediately sat down to check her out on all social media platforms.

"She seems fun," Emily determined, scrolling through photos. There were pictures of friends, prom dates, outdoor adventures.

"Stop!" I cried, leaning over my daughter's shoulder. Emily brought into focus an image of her future dorm-mate in an electric boat on a little lake. "That looks like Westlake Village. Heidi and Martin live there!"

Emily looked at me uninterestedly.

"They send a Christmas card every year. Remember? One of their daughters usually writes the letter...?"

"Mom, Keylynn lives in Thousand Oaks."

"That's not far," I assured her. "Maybe they know each other!"

"There are *lots* of people in California, Mom."

"Yes, there are," I conceded, choosing not to take offense at her dismissive tone. "But you never know. Our friends are Christians. If she's a Christian, they *might* know each other."

"I doubt it."

We hadn't kept in good touch with Heidi and Martin since leaving California some sixteen years prior. The annual Yuletide greeting and warm wishes were all that we exchanged. Still, I treasured the memories that we had made together while young couples—dinner parties with Joel and Colleen, cocktail cruises on their electric boat, weekends at Catalina on *Renaissance*. The best part of our camaraderie, however, had been its Christian foundation. With seriousness and sincerity, we had wrestled together with matters of spiritual significance—tithing and worship, work and parenting—and we had grown because of it. It had been a sweet season.

"Emily, their oldest daughter is your age! The last time we got together was when you were about six months old." Two kids and graduate school had significantly curtailed our social life after that. "When you Facetime Keylynn this weekend, will you just please ask?"

"Fine."

Emily and Keylynn seemed to hit it off immediately. At least, that was my impression of the muffled exchange that I could detect from behind Emily's closed bedroom door. When she finally emerged from her magical kingdom, her face shone with elation.

"Mom! Keylynn's so great!" Emily raved. "She loves camping and hiking.... I was worried that a Christian school might attract nerds, you know, but she's cool." I sensed relief in her voice.

"That's wonderful, Lovey. I'm so glad."

"You know what's crazy, Mom?" Emily asked coyly.

"What?"

"Keylynn *does* know Heidi and Martin *and* their daughter."

"Really? How?!"

"They actually know each other *very well*. Heidi was Keylynn's girls' Bible study leader for *six years*."

I shook my head in amazement.

Was this what Heaven would be like?

"How very exciting," I acknowledged, sending up a silent prayer of thanksgiving. "I think it's going to be a great year."

POETIC PROVISION

Alexander was about to begin his third year of college. The plan was for he and I to drive SallyAnn the Suburban across the country so that our son could finally have a car in Nashville, where he had chosen to go to school. If our old Chevy made the trip, she would end her days in Music City. If she didn't, at least I would be there—with a credit card boasting a larger credit limit than Alexander's—to ensure that he arrived in time for the start of classes.

Deciding on a route, I noticed that we could go through North Dakota, one-time state of residency of Jay and Joan. Indeed, the address that I had for them would be the perfect place to stop after a long first day's drive.

I wondered if they were still there. It had been years since I had spoken with Joan. The thought of seeing them again, of thanking them again for their part in my salvation, was simply too great an enticement. So as not to put any pressure on them to accept our request, I decided to send a note via email.

Joan responded with her characteristic zeal.

"We would *love* to see you and meet your son. Please plan on staying with us."

It seemed surreal that I had first met Jay and Joan when I was younger than our son was now. Where would I be had their path not crossed mine? Lost, more likely than not. Adrift. Far from God.

It was to be, for me, a poignant reunion.

We loaded up the car with Alexander's things: clothing, a mattress, Uncle Don's old dresser, a tennis racket, a soccer ball, a sleeping bag, and a make-shift desk comprised of two sawhorses and a rectangular plywood slab. Alexander and I set out one August morning before dawn.

"Dear Lord," Daniel prayed for us in the driveway. "Please watch over them. Your world is so great and we are so small."

"Amen."

We hugged him goodbye and headed out. I drove. Alexander, who had just rolled out of bed, promptly fell back asleep in the passenger seat. Soon, the eastern horizon began to emerge as light invaded the night sky. It crept up stealthfully, steadily, until finally, the great ball of fire burst over the mighty mountains.

I marveled my way through Montana: the big sky, the Rockies, Ponderosa Pines and tamaracks, ranches and farms, rivers and plains. Heeding Daniel's admonition, I slowed our speed to 60 miles per hour over several mountain passes—including the Continental Divide—and kept my eye on the temperature gauge.

Alexander finally awoke just before noon. Nostalgic already about the summer, likely his last with us, he spoke of his goals and aspirations, his plans and dreams for the future. I soaked up the precious, privileged moments with our son. Then, windows down in the afternoon heat (with no A/C), we listened to music—country and pop and classic rock. We rolled through North Dakota's outstretched fields, plains, and oil pumps to arrive, at last, at our destination around dinnertime.

Emerging from their home, Jay and Joan greeted me timidly but affectionately. While Jay moved more slowly than he had some 25 years earlier, they were little changed from my memory of them. I introduced them to Alexander, who shook their hands warmly. We spoke briefly of the day's journey, the heat and fatigue of driving. Then, offering shelter from the late summer sun, our hosts invited us inside.

Their neat and modest home was full of farm-style decorations, arts and crafts, Christian decor. Eight by ten-inch school portraits of their handsome children adorned the walls. After Joan showed us where to drop our things, we reconvened around the familiar dining room table.

Over supper, we spoke about Jay and Joan's children and grandchildren, their local church, Wells and his family, me and mine. They asked Alexander about his plans (to finish college and, likely, pursue songwriting in Nashville) and queried me about those of our daughter (about to begin college in California). We talked about my work and about my sadness over our imminent empty nest.

Joan commiserated. She, too, had grieved the absence of children in her home. Sensing my chest tighten with emotion, I quickly changed the subject.

"What about you?" I asked Jay. "Are you still in construction?"

Jay shook his head. "No, I haven't been doing that for a while now."

I cringed. Financial struggles had seemed to plague them.

"Jay's back is bad, Bendi, from years of building houses," Joan explained.

I nodded sympathetically, hoping that our presence—and Alexander's impressive appetite—were not a burden.

The air in the room became heavy. I racked my brain for a new subject of conversation.

Jay and Joan gazed at each other tenderly.

"So it's been a blessing" she resumed, "that he hasn't *had* to work these past few years."

"Oh, yeah?" I held my breath in suspense.

"Ever since they found oil on my dad's land."

"They found oil on your dad's land?!"

"Oh, didn't I tell you?" Joan looked to me, her face aglow. "About five years ago. They found oil underneath Dad's farm. Isn't that wonderful?" She patted her husband's worn hand on the table. "Jay will never have to do construction again."

NURTURE AND NATURE

Abeautiful late-summer morning, the sky was clear and blue. I drove, windows down. The still-cool air swirled around my shoulders.

I had just returned from dropping Alexander at his third year of college and Emily at her first. Our home was empty now. The only messes to pick up would be my own.

Daisy tapped the back window with her paw and I opened it. She, too, seemed to miss the busy bustle of the house when the kids were in it, the extra hands to play tug-of-war with her favorite rope, the occasional wrestling session on the floor. When not following me around ruefully, she searched for them in their rooms, in the back yard, among the children passing in the street. Her soulful brown eyes seemed to probe mine for the answer to the same question I kept asking myself.

Now what?

What could I possibly do that would ever be as meaningful as raising children?

Before they were born, I kept reminding myself, I had had goals and dreams and even some pastimes. I had been disciplined and single-minded in my pursuits. How was it that after their arrival, everything changed?

Hearing my phone ding, I glanced at the screen. No text from the kids. Just a work email. Alas.

I smiled remembering Alexander's text after dropping me at the airport where I would fly to join Daniel and Emily at her freshman orientation only the week before.

"I love you mom."

"I love you, too," I had replied—unable to neglect punctuation—even in texts. Tears streamed down my cheeks.

Between the baggage check-in and the security screening, I had managed to lose my boarding pass and needed to return to the ticket counter.

"I just drove my son across the country and I'm leaving him here," I had said by way of explanation. If everything worked out, he would never live in our home again.

"It's a great town," the man had reassured me. "The people are nice." Then, handing me a new ticket: "He'll be fine."

Of course he'll be fine, I thought. It wasn't him that I was worried about.

Alexander had called me then. How ironic—my son checking on me.

"Yes, Lovey, don't worry about me. Are you driving?"

"Yes, Mom."

"Is it legal to talk on the phone without Bluetooth in Tennessee?"

"Yes, Mom."

"Good. Well, thank you for calling, but don't worry. I'll be fine."

"I know, Mom."

"It's just gonna take me a little while..."

It was only natural that it would take a little while. It had taken me a while to get used to the idea of having kids in the first place. Then it had taken me a while to get used to taking care of them. All.the.time. The process of subsuming my plans and desires and career—my life—for the sake of the kids, for the sake of our family, had required tremendous effort.

I was evidently not very good at transitions.

Daisy put her head between the front seats for a little pat. I willingly obliged.

Ahead on the rural road, a spill of popcorn blew over the pavement. Or was it leaves? I watched enchanted as a funnel of air swirled them around bewitchingly. It wasn't until I saw a dove-like bird weaving in and around the miniature tumbleweeds that I recognized that it was neither leaves nor tumbleweeds but a family of quails.

I slammed on the brakes—sending our dog toppling into the back of my seat. Tires screeched. Rubber burned.

Still, the confused hen ran toward the car.

Was she blind?

Would I stop in time?!

I braced myself against the steering wheel and squeezed my eyes shut.

At last at rest in the narrow lane, I wondered what I would find on the pavement. I dreaded the thought.

Still, I couldn't stay where I was. I had to go on, had to look.

And there, just a few feet from my bumper, stood the mother quail. Alive and valiant and resolute. Before her, beneath her legs, cowered a wayward chick that she had run to "protect."

The winged mother and I stared at each other for a quick second, my blurred gaze of admiration saluting her. Then she whisked away her errant brood.

I put the car in park in the middle of the road, tried to calm my racing heart. It had all passed so quickly.

The little birds flown away.

TRAMPOLINES AND UMBRELLAS

"Take turns jumping on the trampoline."

I had thought it a strange inscription for a wedding card. But someone had written it on ours more than 20 years prior. And unlike the other "normal" wishes, it had stuck with me.

I had certainly jumped! And I was thankful that Daniel had encouraged it. Most days, I recognized him for the blessing that he was.

That day, I did not.

Since moving to the Northwest some dozen years prior, Daniel had struggled with Season Affective Disorder. Whether due to the many days of overcast skies or the less than nine hours of daylight we enjoyed during *two long months* each winter, my husband had been negative and dejected of late, moody and listless.

And I was sick of it.

Tired of the negativity. Tired of the bickering. Tired of it all.

Such was the focus of my thoughts when I set out on a run one day. Emily and I had decided to sign up for a half-marathon. Since she was now away at college, the thrill was simply the opportunity to think of her, and hope that she might be thinking of me. We would send each other Snaps of our course of the day and discuss, over the phone, our progress in terms of speed or distance. Mostly, it was nice to know that someone else was suffering.

I was not really a runner. I had jogged off and on over the years, even finished the marathon with some friends several years earlier, but running was not something that I enjoyed. Less time-consuming than a hike or a trip to the gym, it was simply an efficient way to stay in shape. So I endured it.

For any distance longer than about a mile, however, I relied heavily on music. Training for the half-marathon in hopes of keeping up with Emily, I had spent some time putting together a playlist that would increase my speed—a faster song followed by a slower song. It was all about beats-per-minute, getting my legs to move, interspersed with a little recovery time.

That day, it felt good to run. Maybe it was the frustration.

I was improving myself.

The air in my lungs felt energizing. Restorative.

Daniel wasn't improving himself. He was at home grumbling.

Music boosted me, though this particular song struck me as annoying: a male rapper was accompanied by a female singer who was grunting vowel sounds. I made a mental note to review the playlist, when I was not trying to keep the pace, and remove irritating songs like this one.

I'm sick of the gloominess.

The beat of the music pulsed in my ears. I pushed my legs to keep up.

You've got this. You can do anything for three minutes.

I turned up the volume to distract me from the pain:

Ella ella eh eh eh.

Under my umbrella. Ella ella eh eh.

Under my umbrella. Ella ella eh eh eh.

Under my umbrella. Ella ella eh eh eh eh eh eh.

You can run into my arms.

It's okay, don't be alarmed.

Come here to me.

There's no distance in between our love.

So go on and let the rain pour.

I'll be all you need and more...

Though I had definitely heard the song before, I had never *listened* to the lyrics before that day, never heard the noble message they contained.

I wondered if Rihanna was married, quickly decided that she likely was not.

The song continued:

Because when the sun shines we'll shine together.

Told you I'd be here forever.

Said I'll always be your friend.

Took an oath, I'mma stick it out 'til the end.

Now that it's raining more than ever

Know that we'll still have each other.

You can stand under my umbrella.

You can stand under my umbrella...

I couldn't believe my ears: "An oath," "we'll have each other," "you can stand under my umbrella."

Was God really going to use a pop song to convict me of my selfishness? Sheesh!

I slowed my pace to a walk and paused the playlist. I needed to catch my breath and consider what the Lord was trying to show me. The message was, in my headphones, loud and clear.

I was a fool. A self-centered, egotistical fool.

Daniel had made a sacrifice to come to the States, something that I had not considered at age 21. Far from his family, his culture, everything that was familiar, he had had to start over, at 28, with a new language, new friends, a new way of life to be with me.

Daniel had been supportive of my decision to return to graduate school, at the cost of years of my time—*our* time—and *more* student loans.

Daniel had been willing to make the move north to be closer to my family, at the expense of his good job in Los Angeles.

My husband had not only let me jump on the trampoline, he had allowed me to soar. He had, moreover, been my umbrella during many a storm: bringing us safely to anchor at sea, comforting me during the years of grieving Mom—the fetal-position-sob-sessions-on-the-floor years, heartening me in our current transition to empty-nesthood...

Daniel was a good husband. A good father. A good man. We could work through this challenge—as we had so many others—together.

Thus the Lord reminded me of the vow that I had taken some twenty years prior: "For better or for worse." It was a covenant that I had made not only with Daniel but with Him.

And I would keep my promise.

A DIVINE APPOINTMENT

During Emily's first year at college, I was—beginning in January—granted a sabbatical from teaching. It was a blessing to have extended time to read and write and rejuvenate.

Yet I was having a hard time getting out of bed in the morning.

What's the point? I reasoned. No one needed me—not my kids, not my students. And while Daniel enjoyed my company, he could very capably take care of himself.

Recognizing my quasi-depression, I determined to oblige myself to get out of the house. I needed to feel useful, helpful, needed. So I applied to be a substitute teacher at the local high schools. I filled out the application, paid for the fingerprinting and background check, requested references, and even went through the training.

"There are other options, Mom," Alexander insisted on the phone. "You don't want to do that to yourself."

Reflecting on some of the bad behavior of my own high school years—including a classmate convincing our entire algebra class to lean left fifteen degrees to see if Mrs. Anderson, who suffered with Multiple Sclerosis, would lose her balance and end instruction early—I reluctantly agreed.

So I decided to volunteer for women's ministry at our church. Over the years, I had been involved in one Bible study or another—whether leading Emily and her elementary school classmates or hosting a diverse assortment of friends and neighbor ladies at our home. But while the kids were still around, I had been hesitant to take on the weightier weekly responsibility of volunteering in such a capacity at church.

A new day had dawned.

I called our megachurch and left a message. I felt a sense of urgency—not only because of the dark days of January, but—because there were only a few months during which I could volunteer on Tuesday mornings before I would return again to teaching. Impatient for a reply, I also called Maribeth, a friend whom I knew had served in such a role in the past. Maribeth passed along my contact information to Tina, the head of women's ministry, who phoned one evening after dinner.

"Hello."

"Hello! It's Tina from church."

"Hi, Tina. Thanks for the call."

"Of course! Maribeth mentioned that you might be able to help in women's ministry."

"I would really like that!"

We spoke about my interest in leading a Bible study, my past experiences facilitating groups, my longevity at the church. Sweetly and shrewdly, Tina interviewed me for the "job." As our conversation drew to a close, she turned to logistics.

"I also want to give you the number of another woman in leadership," Tina explained, "since I'll be transitioning out of this position within the next few months."

"Oh really?"

"Yes, my husband and I have felt led by the Lord to move to Fiji to train church leaders there."

"Wow! That's exciting!"

"We *are* excited," Tina admitted, "but also a little nervous to trade the known for the unknown."

"Of course," I acknowledged. "When will you be leaving?"

"At the end of July."

"Well, I can only help through the beginning of August anyway, since I'll need to go back to work after that. "

"What do you do, Bendi?"

"I'm a French professor."

"Oh *really?*" Tina seemed particularly impressed.

"Yeah, I love it. Getting to know students, constantly learning...I just love it."

"I'd like to talk more about this with you in person."

"Sure," I shrugged. "I'd be happy to." Then, reminding me of the date of the official orientation meeting, Tina wished me a good evening.

Within a few weeks, women's Bible study classes recommenced at Real Life Ministries.[1] The ladies in my group had been sharing with transparency, sharpening each other and sharpening me. I was blessed to be a part. Committed to be present each week, to prepare for each lesson through the study of God's Word, and to pray for the women between gatherings, I also felt useful, helpful, and, to some degree, needed. I was reminded yet again that, "It is more blessed to give than to receive."[2]

I was setting up my classroom for what would be the fourth session of the excellent and utterly convicting study *Lord, Change my Attitude* by James McDonald when Tina entered the room. A tall man lingered just behind her in the doorway.

"Good morning, Bendi!" she beamed as she scooped me in for a hug. Then, turning to the door, she gestured toward her companion. "Bendi, I wanted to introduce you to my husband, Dave."

Dave stepped into the room. I extended my hand and we shook.

"Nice to meet you."

I wondered why Tina thought that I needed to meet Dave right then; the chairs and tables were not yet set up.

"Bendi, we wanted to talk to you about something."

"Sure," I replied, now concerned that I must have somehow offended a woman in my group. *Was this a Matthew 18 moment? What had I said to upset someone?* My palms started to sweat. "Did I do something wrong, Tina?"

"Oh, no, no, Bendi," Tina assured me. "It's nothing like that."

I exhaled, relieved.

"Here," Dave grabbed some chairs, "let's sit down."

We arranged ourselves into a little triangle. Tina looked to Dave as if to prompt him. I glanced at the clock—twelve minutes until the ladies would arrive. Tick Tick...I tried a variation of my Lamaze breathing. *Breathe. Relax.* As during childbirth, it didn't work.

At last, Dave broke the silence.

"So Tina told you about our plan to move to Fiji?"

"She did! It sounds very exciting." I spoke with sincerity, always interested in the health and vibrancy of the Church around the globe. I always enjoyed attending services outside of my home faith community—in the U.S. and abroad—meeting brothers and sisters in Christ with whom I would share eternity.

"Yes, we are excited," Dave began. "They bring in leaders from all over the South Pacific for trainings. We've visited several times. This last trip, we just really felt like the Lord wanted us to be there." Dave reached for Tina's hand. Still smiling, Tina's gaze oscillated from her husband to me.

"How cool to be part of what the Lord is doing in another part of the world!" I hoped that they could sense my admiration for their faith, their courage, and their willingness to submit to God's call.

"It is," he nodded, eyes aglow. Dave leaned in a little now, as if taking me into his confidence. "We wanted to ask a favor of you, Bendi."

"Yes, of course."

Were they here to request financial support?

"Please don't feel obligated," Dave continued, "but Tina says that you know *French*."

"I *do*." I replied, intrigued.

"Our friend from Fiji is moving to New Caledonia where they'll be using our church's discipleship manual in the Bible college there. They speak French in New Caledonia, in Tahiti, and on some neighboring islands. We're trying to learn the language, but it's difficult, you know, after a certain age to master a new tongue."

"It is," I agreed.

Was it tutoring they wanted?

"And the materials that we have, that our church publishes, they're all in English."

I nodded, still not certain what they were asking.

"We were wondering, Bendi, if you would be willing to translate the discipleship training manual into French."

I smiled at the Lord's provision, his timing, his care.

Useful. Helpful. Needed.

"I would be honored," I said decisively. "Truly. I would be honored to help."

PREACH!

"**M**om," Alexander began, "I have a funny story for you."

Now in his senior year of college, our son phoned a couple times each week. I looked forward to our conversations.

"Remember how I sent a text to Zach and he didn't respond?"

"Zach, your old roommate?"

"No. Remember...the son of your colleague, the kid who's a year older than me?"

"Oh, *that* Zach. Yes, I remember. That was a long time ago, wasn't it?"

"Yeah, I texted him the summer before coming to Nashville to see if we could meet up."

Alexander hadn't known anyone in Tennessee. Learning that one of my associates had a child attending the same institution, I had asked for the boy's number and passed it along to Alexander. Our son had reached out in hopes of making a friend—or, at least, of having a familiar face that he might recognize on campus. Zach had initially responded saying that he didn't have a means of transportation. But when Alexander suggested a few dates that he could travel to Zach, Zach never replied.

"Maybe he was just shy or uncomfortable getting together with a someone he'd never met," I offered, trying—for the umpteenth time—to lessen the sting.

"Yeah, yeah," Alexander interrupted dismissively. "Just listen!"

I paced our living room, some two thousand miles away, awaiting the upshot of the Zach saga.

"I was a little miffed when he didn't respond," Alexander resumed. "I wasn't expecting to be best friends or anything. But it would've been nice to know someone, you know, even to be able to ask some questions."

"I know..."

"I had looked him up on social media so I recognized him when I saw him on campus a few times."

"Did you introduce yourself?"

"Of course not! If he wasn't even willing to get together when we were home, why would I bug him here?"

"I guess..."

"He's an aspiring artist. He actually played at a party I attended once. When we were there, I told Henry what had happened—or didn't happen."

"And?"

"Henry tried to convince me to fight him."

"Oh, my goodness!"

"He's not very big."

"You wouldn't do that...would you?"

"No, Mom, I wouldn't. But we had had a couple of beers so I thought about it for a minute."

I was getting nervous. I hoped that my associate did not rue the day that she gave me her son's number.

"So what happened?! Finish your story!"

"Well, I was at work the other day on campus. There wasn't anything that they needed me to do so I started cleaning out my computer. I had a ton of text messages to go through."

"Text messages on your computer?"

"I have my texts sync automatically. Then, I can delete things on my phone to save memory."

"I didn't know you could do that. Okay."

"Guess what I found?"

"You didn't..."

"I did. A reply from Zach—from *four years ago*."

"Oh, bummer," I sighed. "Well, I'm glad you found it."

"Me too."

"You should respond to him."

Alexander was quiet on the other end of the line.

"Are you going to respond to him?"

"I dunno," our son hesitated. "A lot of time has passed."

Clenching my fists, I fought to hold my tongue. *When was it exactly that parents were supposed to cease telling their kids what they should do?* I still hadn't found that passage in the Bible. Alas.

Alexander groaned into the receiver. At last.

"I guess it's the right thing to do," he admitted.

"It is."

Our son exhaled deeply. I could almost hear the cogitations bubbling in his brain.

"This is actually pretty convicting, Mom."

"What do you mean?"

"Well, not only was I thinking bad things about someone—even saying things about him that weren't correct—but when it came time for me to do what I was blaming him for *not* doing, I didn't want to do it."

Why do you look at the speck of sawdust in your brother's eye and pay no attention to the plank in your own eye? How can you say to your brother, 'Let me take the speck out of your eye,' when all the time there is a plank in your own eye? You hypocrite, first take the plank out of your own eye, and then you will see clearly to remove the speck from your brother's eye.[1]

"Life is humbling, isn't it?"

"It is." Alexander conceded, his tone contemplative. "When I think about it, it could've been a sermon."

Indeed.

KNOWN AND LOVED

Rays of dawn poured in from the sunroof as I drove to work. An exceptional playlist of Christian songs succeeded each other on the radio. Flocks of birds flitted here and there, circling and diving as if choreographed to the music coming from my speakers.

God was showing off.

Praise You, Lord.

I laughed as another of my favorite melodies started to play. Dabbing the tears from my cheeks, I decided that I should really keep a tube of mascara in my purse.

All of creation was waking up. The trees, heavy with buds, seemed to burst with color. Brave daffodils rose above the still cold ground; their yellow faces shone with expectancy. The creatures of the sky warbled in joy at the hope of the new day.

Watching their playful flight, I thought of my grandmother. She had always loved birds. A former librarian, she had collected several books about them. Grandma would sit for hours at her dining room table overlooking the bird bath and bird box and bird feeders in the backyard, identifying the familiar species and looking up new ones.

"Do you see that one, Dear?" she'd point excitedly. "That's a Western Meadowlark. Just look at his striking yellow breast, his little black bib."

"Cute."

"His song is beautiful, too!"

At age ten and twelve and fifteen, I had not been interested in birds. Sure, I would watch a pretty blue jay bathe in the stone urn on her patio, his tiny head dipping into the water, his whole body convulsing to fluff his majestic cerulean feathers. But linger and study and even redesign bird feeders so as to avoid bully birds, never!

I shook my head at the memory and mused at the twist of fate. Now, it was I who paused to watch birds drink and bathe in our fountain. It was I who attempted to lure hummingbirds with our red glass feeder. I had even recently taken an interest in birds' courtship habits. How ironic.

Grandma had wanted a chickadee on her tombstone. Those friendly, non-migratory birds had kept her company many a day. We decided on a twig-bearing dove for Mom—a symbol of nest-making, of home, and of peace. Dad, for his stone, had chosen a goose in flight.

How I missed them all.

My current bird of choice—besides my all-time favorite, the hummingbird, a true masterwork of the Lord—was the hawk. This bird of prey also made appearances on my commute—often sitting in the same location day after day. His keen eye was focused; his intensity, evident. Was it his sharpness that I admired? He was known to be intelligent. No, I think it was his speed, his power. I loved the initial burst of force from his great wings as he took flight. I loved the way that he soared effortlessly. His cousin, the Peregrine falcon, was known to be the fastest creature on earth—able to reach speeds over 200 miles per hour! Pretty amazing for a little bird.

A hawk, however, would probably not be the best thing to have engraved on my tombstone. I giggled imagining the reactions of those who might visit my grave.

"I never knew Bendi to be a violent person."

"She wasn't a good hunter, that's for sure."

"Bendi always did strike me as a little aloof."

The only fowl that might be funnier to etch on a grave marker would be Daisy's nemesis, the turkey. Though our dog had chased a few silly gobblers into trees while still a puppy, she now feared them more than a missed meal. Perhaps it was their habit of traveling in large flocks around our neighborhood. Or maybe it was the vertical proximity of their beaks to her eyes. Whatever the reason, Daisy wanted nothing to do with these bald, babbling beasts.

I vowed not to give Emily, my future funeral director, any ideas.

The birds had continued to play all around me: swooping, gliding, weaving a wondrous whirlpool in the sky. One would've thought that I had installed a birdfeeder on my roof.

And then, calamity struck. A little bird—was it a sparrow?—flew directly into the path of my car. Traveling quickly with vehicles all around me, I could do nothing to avoid it. I hit the tiny creature full force. It dropped, lifeless, to the pavement.

I was sickened. Horrified. The poor little bird.

I'm sorry, Lord.

Yet even while praying, I realized that God could've changed the bird's flight. Why then had He allow it to happen? He knew how much I loved those little creatures. I had, in fact, just been admiring them, celebrating his amazing creativity as observed in the winged splendor of the sky.

I turned off the radio to drive in silence. I felt offended. Hurt. I clenched my jaw and wiped my eyes.

My mom had once accidentally hit a chicken crossing the road. (Really.) She had cried and cried over the silly thing. And I had not understood it.

And yet this seemed different. It was different—I was sure of it. I felt like God was trying to show me something.

The sun, now higher in the sky, warmed the top of my head. I basked in the glow. It had been a long winter.

He was a good God, I knew. I decided to bring my question to Him. I approached at last, humbly, reverently.

Lord, why did you allow that to happen? You know how I love the little birds.

The answer came quickly, so quickly that I was sure that it was Him.

"Are not two sparrows sold for a penny? Yet not one of them will fall to the ground outside your Father's care"[1]; "You are of more value than many sparrows"[2]; "Even the hairs of your head are all numbered."[3]

I smiled. I had a lot of hair.

So kind, He was. So very kind. I had been upset, troubled by the well-being of a small bird. A small bird whose significance mattered even to Lord and Creator of the universe.

Yet God had allowed me to feel compassion and concern for one of his creatures so that, by degrees, He could grant me a small glimpse of a love, compassion, and concern infinitely greater.

The love that He has for me.

WAITING TABLES IN NASHVILLE

Alexander had graduated from college. We were so proud.

Our son, on the other hand, was uneasy. His post-graduation steps would be the first in his life that hadn't been laid out for him—elementary school preceded middle school, followed by high school, and then college. Now, on the other side of the country, far from family, Alexander had reached the end of the known. There was no guidebook for "How to Make It as an Artist/Songwriter."[1] His future success would require improvisation, networking, and a lot of hard work.

And our generally serene, level-headed, competent, go-getter son was terrified.

How long would family, who had always supported him in his musical endeavors, continue to encourage him toward this dream?

What would his friends, many of whom had accepted jobs that came with insurance and retirement accounts, think of his decision?

How would his newish girlfriend feel about the vocational pursuits of an aspiring singer-songwriter who was currently waiting tables to pay the rent?

"You know, Mom, if you guys didn't believe in me so much, I would've probably taken a regular job." He sounded almost angry. He sounded scared.

"We do believe in you, Lovey. Your songs are *good*."

"It's just...it's just that it would've been *easier* to do something else."

"Sure," I agreed. "But little that is *easy* in life is worthwhile." I thought of relationships, marriage, motherhood, work. I prayed that the Lord would bring along little signs of encouragement for our son.

"You've got this, Lovey."

Just days after returning from Nashville, I was on the phone with a colleague at work. An award-winning teacher and impressive scholar, Adam was one of the most admired professors on campus. He was also wise and humble and kind. We knew each other's families a bit from having visited on the sidelines of our daughters' high school soccer games. His girl had played against mine.

"How is your family?" I asked after working out the details of an honors student's independent study. Adam spoke of his daughters with delight and affection. There had been physical injuries and spiritual triumphs. They were growing in maturity and in faith.

"What about your kids?" he countered.

"Emily just finished her second year of college. She's thinking law school."

"Is she playing soccer? I can't remember."

"Only intramurals," I replied, reminiscing on her recent text about a boy on the soccer team who had run her over. ("He was trash-talking me and everything, Mom, like an equal! Afterwards, he apologized—said that he'd thought that I would flinch.") A real pistol, that Emily. I loved her grit.

"And what's your son doing now?" Adam asked.

I paused, wondering how much to say, wondering how Alexander would want me to respond.

"Alexander just graduated!" I cheered. "He decided to stay in Nashville, to work in the music industry. He's a little nervous about it—about the fact that even though he earned a degree, he is, at age 22, waiting tables so that he has time to work on his music."

"That's great, Bendi," Adam responded kindly. I was appreciative once again of his humanity, his grace.

"You know what I did after college?" Adam resumed.

"No," I played along. "What did you do?"

"I waited tables in Nashville."

"Really?"

"Really."

I smiled.

"Thanks, Adam. I'll be sure to tell him."

NEW LIFE

Stewart invited Emily to be a leader at the Young Life camp in Malibu, British Columbia. We had known Stewart for years. A successful businessman, Stewart also served as the assistant soccer coach at Emily's high school. He was, moreover, the sponsor of Young Life on the Jesuit campus. The man was, in a word, a saint.

"I don't know if I should do it, Mom," Emily explained. "I'd have to take time off work."

"Mmm..."

"Plus, it costs $500."

"Leaders have to pay?!"

"For food and transportation."

"That's ridiculous," I said.

Summer was money-making season for Emily. Though we helped her through school, we expected her to cover a significant percentage of her university expenses. Plus, Emily hoped to finally bring a car to campus next year, her third in college. And while we would contribute to that as well, she had a long way to go to be able to purchase something that was not going to be a lemon. Attending the Young Life Camp would mean not only less summer earnings for her but an additional expense for us.

Emily raised the matter again a few days later, her tone altered.

"It would probably be the last time I'd ever go to summer camp."

"Is that a good reason?"

Emily was not amused.

"I think I should do it, Mom. Stewart needs leaders and I believe I could do a good job."

I began to feel guilty for discounting a potentially eternity-changing week.

"Yes, I'm sure that you would do a good job," I acknowledged.

"What if I wrote letters to friends and family asking for support?" she suggested.

I didn't like the idea of hitting up friends and family members for a *summer camp*. Still, I had to admit that the cost of Emily's participation was a significant reservation. Between the final payments for Alexander's education, our family trip to attend his graduation, Emily's school costs, and some medical expenses, our bank account had been hard hit of late. I sighed.

"You could do that, I guess."

And with that, it was decided.

Over the next several weeks, Emily attended regular leader meetings hosted by Stewart. Over pizza or tacos or Oreo milkshakes, she learned the vision of Young Life's founder, the mission statement of the organization, and the methods Young Life employs to win souls for Christ. She participated in the parent orientation meeting and other pre-camp events intended to introduce campers and leaders—meet-and-greets, frozen yogurt nights, and lake days.

Emily was getting excited about the prospect of introducing kids to Jesus.

"Did you know that Young Life is one of the only Christian organizations that goes to kids—like to watch their theatre performances or sit with them on the bleachers at football games?"

"I'd never thought about that."

"Yeah, and did you know that Stewart's business pays part of the cost for the kids from our high school to attend camp?"

"No, I didn't know that."

"Other high schoolers in the area have to pay two hundred dollars more to go."

"Oh, my!"

"Stewart said that when it's too much for his business or if he's running short, he reaches out to Young Life alumni in the area and they pitch in."

I smiled at the example of the body of Christ working together.

"He told me he'll probably be calling me in the future," Emily laughed.

She was catching a glimpse of it: a faith that extended way beyond herself. The dedication and sacrifice of Stewart, the generosity of God's people—including many who donated to her week at camp—all worked toward the goal of saving the lost. Emily was beginning to see her place in it.

She taped the list of her campers to the bathroom mirror and committed to pray for them.

Departure day finally came. Emily, who (unless it was her birthday) never picked up the mail from our box down the street, rushed into my room where I was getting ready. In her hand, she waved one last check.

"That's it, Mom! It's all covered!"

Having long believed that we had seen the last of the contributions, I shook my head in amazement. "That's wonderful, Dolly. The Lord is so kind."

Picking up our daughter at their dawn arrival from camp, I took us to a nearby coffee shop. I wanted the unabridged, caffeine-infused debrief of her week at Malibu.

With steaming mugs and breakfast treats in hand, we made it to a window table.

"Tell me everything!"

"Oh, Mom. It was *amazing*!" Emily began. She talked about the camp's majestic location, its awe-inspiring views. She enthused over the many activities: games, outdoor recreation, challenge courses, music, messages, and quiet time—all planned with intentionality in order to lead kids to Christ. She shared about the wonderful camaraderie of the Young Life staff, the continued training that she received as a leader, the inspiring devotional times for those serving. And she spoke lovingly—showing me picture after picture—of the girls in her cabin: their dearness and tenderness, their struggles and strife.

"And Mom!" Emily gasped, having spoken for an hour while barely taking a breath. "*Five* of the girls gave their lives to Christ! *Five girls!*" Tears streamed down her cheeks.

"Hallelujah!" I rejoiced, wiping my own face.

Thankful for the God of mercy and grace.

The God who provides.

The God who blesses us with the privilege of being a small part.

IT IS WELL

Because of the generous hospitality of extended family, I had grown up in lakefront homes. Few earthly pastimes trump swimming and boating on a mountain lake, sunning lazily on a private dock, making s'mores and tale tale-telling around a campfire. Years and years of treasured memories—many of which included my mom or dad—had convinced me of the singular status of a place on the lake.

So after paying my student loans, with the little money Mom left us, Daniel and I had put a down payment on a modest cottage on a nearby lake. The one-bedroom cabin sat underneath a majestic cedar, which created a perfect canopy in the heat of the summer for our open-air dining "room." We would linger in the cool grass for hours enjoying food, conversation, and views of the pristine lake. A rustic, rock fireplace sat just behind the table to border the property line with the undeveloped lot to our West. The inside of the cabin was just as quaint. Cedar planking lined the walls and ceiling. The grooves from the first owner's rocking chair marked one corner of the original hardwood floor. A squeaky sliding door opened to a rickety deck, which offered another vista from which to admire the Lord's handiwork—Ponderosa and Northern Pine, eagles and osprey, ducks and geese.

We swam and boated; we played board games and ping pong; we dealt cards and built campfires. The kids, still young at the time, had not always appreciated the quiet and disconnected nature of our days at the lake. We had no television, no video game console, no computer or Internet access. We had, moreover, few extended family members with whom to make memories. Alexander and Emily had complained about "missing out" on friends and in-town activities. They had also rued the long hours required to open the cabin in the spring and close it in the fall.

To help pay the mortgage, we had sublet it as a weekly vacation rental. I blocked off three weeks each year for us to enjoy—beginning with the 4th of July. Yet, inevitably, at least one of these weeks would be rainy and cold. I had served as cleaning lady in between guests—washing dishes and cleaning floors, scrubbing bathrooms and changing sheets, refreshing towels and hauling away garbage. It was a lot of work, work that became stressful when guests scheduled to leave by 11 a.m. did not, and the next boarders arrived at 3 p.m.

Four years into this battle we had reluctantly sold our bungalow and, at my prompting, reinvested the equity in a piece of land on the lake closer to town. This location would allow us to live there year-round. My commute to work would be just a little over an hour. It would all be worth it, I was convinced, to enjoy the view of God's creation from that perspective. Even more importantly, a house on the lake would serve as a lure to draw our adult children—and, we prayed, our future grandchildren—back home.

Eight years had passed. We had paid off the lot. So in September, with Alexander now out of college, we began at last to work on the project of building.

The property was steep and the building footprint, small. Our first step was to request a variance from the county. Our builder kindly filled out the paperwork. We then waited six months as the county gathered information from pertinent agencies. Neighbors were also invited to weigh in on our request. Confident that, given the challenges of the lot and our modest demand, the variance would be approved, we did not even prepare any remarks for the judge.

Our request was denied.

"I should've put together a stronger proposal," our builder apologized, "but I'm sure it will go through. I'll just have to do a better job next time." We requested a review, paid the additional fee, and waited for the next meeting with the county commissioners.

At our second variance hearing, the out-of-state neighbors who spent just three months each year at their lakefront home (while our lot required us to build on the other side of the road—behind them—meaning that no inch of their view would be impacted from our request) sent a lawyer to argue against our bid. Given this firepower, we were thankful to win a *portion* of our initial request.

It was now April.

Hopeful that we might begin the process of building that summer, we started to apply for financing. To avoid the high fees associated with a construction loan, we applied for a home equity line, promising to roll it into a mortgage when we sold our residence. While the bank ordered a home appraisal, we supplied two years of tax returns, three months of W2s, checking account statements, retirement account statements, and a half-dozen other evidences of our ability to repay.

We received only partial funding.

"Well, I guess we'll have to go with a construction loan," I shrugged.

Daniel and I had been scouring magazines and internet sites for design ideas for years. We now toured appliance outlets, cabinet makers, granite suppliers, and flooring warehouses. Daniel poured over floor plans. A guru for detail, he measured room sizes, hallways, ceiling heights, and garages. He paid attention to practicality, aesthetics, cost. With the meticulousness of an architect, Daniel drafted our new home on 11" x 17" graph paper, purchased expressly for the purpose. These drawings were then turned over to a professional draftsman who drew up the official plans.

Having determined to put our house on the market the following spring, we had a garage sale to get rid of items that we would not want or need in our new home. I took pictures of the yard while the flowers were in bloom and asked a family friend to make a drone video of the neighborhood. I purchased identical hangers to make our closets look more orderly for potential buyers, color-coded our clothing, and changed my work password to "houseonthelake."

Our builder had ordered a geotechnical survey shortly after our variance was approved. The engineers had been so busy with other projects, however, that they were unable to complete a soil sample on our lot before August. We began to doubt the possibility of beginning construction before winter.

Returned from work one Monday afternoon, I found Daniel on the deck. The cool September sunshine traced long shadows on our back lawn. Greeting him with a kiss, I sat down opposite him at our patio table.

"How was your day?"

"Well, I finally heard from the geotech engineer." He sounded glum.

"What did he say?"

"He said that, because of the instability of the land and lack of solid rock, we'll need a second survey."

"Well that's too bad." I realized that this meant that we would definitely not be starting construction in the fall. "So when can they do that?"

"We didn't even get into dates, Bendi. The cost for the next survey would be about ten percent of our total budget for the house."

"Wow," I sighed. Another setback. We had already spent thousands on surveys and applications and blueprints. And we now knew that we would require a structural engineer to boot. Additional costs would certainly cut into the quality of our finishes.

But Daniel had more to say. "The engineer actually suggested that, given the challenges of our lot, it might be better to sell it."

My heart sank.

We sat there for a while in silence. Where would we go from here? The peaceful trickle of the fountain beneath the Japanese maple failed to sooth my stormy spirit.

"We could change the floor plans," Daniel suggested finally. "We could make it a *lot* smaller."

It was hard to imagine how we could host grandkids with less space.

"The goal is to be on the lake, isn't it?"

I sighed deeply, closed my eyes, and fought my raging resolve. Fought to let go of my sense of entitlement.

"Yes, it is," I managed, finally. We would just have to adjust.

On Thursday, Daniel was let go at work. His newest position, which we had considered an answer to prayer, was eliminated because of restructuring.

We were stunned. Dismayed. Shell-shocked.

The house was particularly quiet that evening. The elephant in the room sucked out all the oxygen. Intermittently, clumsily, I tried to comfort my husband who had never before lost a job and who, at 56, now faced the strain of looking for new employment.

Then there was the matter of the house on the lake.

"Maybe God just doesn't want us to build right now," I admitted begrudgingly. We were again on the back deck. The leaves of the Aspen danced quietly in the evening breeze.

"Couldn't He have just *told* us?"

"I think He did." The unsuccessful variance request, the denied loan, the unstable soil, the unexpected loss of income...so many difficulties, so many challenges.

We were each drowning in emotion. I was sad for my husband, heart-sick over the probable end of a childhood dream. Daniel was rattled from the layoff, remorseful for having let me down. Me, the coveter of a house on the lake.

We were gentle with our words that evening, poignantly aware of the fragility of it all. Hand-in-hand, we prayed for wisdom and direction, for clarity on the future that God had for us.

"One thing I know," Daniel said, pulling me toward him in an embrace, "is that—after God—you and the kids are the best thing that ever happened to me."

"Thank you, Love."

"Things like this just put it all in perspective."

"I know. You're right," I nodded, still trying to surrender my spirit to this new possibility, this new future. "I love you." I squeezed Daniel tenderly. "I'm going to go get ready for bed."

Climbing the stairs, I opened a music app on my phone. A little worship would do my soul good. Although I had my favorite artists, my favorite worship songs *du jour,* I generally opted for the radio station shuffle and the pleasure of the unexpected.

Orchestral strings moaned as I entered the bathroom. I turned up the volume. Soon, Lauren Daigle's soulful voice reverberated around the little tile chamber. She, too, sounded like she was grieving.

> "In the darkest hour
> when I cannot breathe,
> fear is on my chest,
> the weight of the world on me."

This isn't a dark hour, Lord, I acknowledged, tears streaming down my face.

Simple chords on a piano accompanied the voice of a worshiper.

"Everything is crashing down,
everything I have known."

I am so blessed, Lord. I know it! My kids are healthy. My husband still loves me.

"When I wonder if I'm all alone,
I remember, I remember:
You have always been faithful to me."

Lauren declared my truth, the truth about which I had been trying these past months to write.

Forgive me for wanting more than the blessings you have showered on me, Lord.

It was only a house on the lake.

I raised my hands, bowed my head, and joined my sister in adoration.

"I remember, I remember:
Even when my own eyes could not see.
You were there, always there
With me."

"I HAVE DRAWN YOU WITH UNFAILING KINDNESS"[1]

On the phone with Alexander, I told him about the challenges we were having with the lot, about Daniel's job. I told him that we might not be able to build on the lake. I narrated quietly, trying to hide the distress that I felt.

"Let's pray about it, Mom."

"Yes," I agreed. "Let's pray."

Then, my 22-year old son knocked on the throne room of Heaven for his dad and me.

And I was struck by the Lord's kindness.

Alexander had attended church with us nearly every week of his first eighteen years. At age eight, he had asked to be baptized, a ceremony that we had accomplished in a hot tub with our home group from church. His summers had always included a Vacation Bible School or a Christian summer camp. Following at least two of these, he had returned having caught a glimpse of the Lord, having "tasted" and seen his goodness.[2] Beginning in elementary school, Alexander had participated in small groups with peers. The first had been with Robert, the father of one of the boys, who had encouraged Alexander to lead worship each week. In middle school, Melaine had organized a slightly different group of boys to meet with Zach, a young man from our church, to talk about God, the Gospel, and girls. In high school, Cody had capably led a Fellowship of Christian Athletes group. There were yet others—Joe and Tofer and Seth.... Dozens of saints had, with intentionality and care, made efforts to connect with our son, to disciple and mentor him in his Christian walk.

So many post-summer camp highs! So many years among people of shared belief! So many faithful servants! And yet, when Alexander had left home for college, he had not yet fully taken on the faith.

Maybe it had been the girlfriend, an outspoken agnostic, who had discouraged him.

Maybe it had been the sanctimoniousness he discerned in many who professed to be Christians.

Maybe it had been the uncompelling witness of us, his parents.

Whatever the reason, Alexander had remained lukewarm.

Consequently, when he had gone away to school, he had not made any effort to get connected with other believers. He didn't set foot in church for *two long years.*

And I had prayed.

Then the summer before his junior year of college, Alexander had faced some difficulty finding a place to live within his (our) price point. At the last minute, he had ended up signing a lease with a group of guys that he barely knew.

"I think they're Christians, Mom."

"Why do you say that?"

"I don't know...the way they talk," he reflected. "They just seem to do different things—like go out less, hang out together more."

It sounded good to me.

"Well, you'll know soon enough."

And, in fact, the four young men were believers, earnest followers of Christ. They invited Alexander to church with them and he went! A couple of them became involved in a ministry for college-aged men,[3] and Alexander joined them. Throughout the year, they even hosted some men's ministry events at their place.

I quietly celebrated the Lord's orchestration of all things.

And then Alexander met a young woman who loved Jesus—a detail that I ascertained both from her Instagram account and the lyrics of one of Alexander's new songs—something about a girl his mom would like.

On the phone, however, our son expressed frustration at what he deemed her unusual behavior.

"She's sweet and she's beautiful, and I like her. I just don't *get* her."

"What do you mean?"

"Well, she, like, she doesn't initiate texts or Snapchats."

"Well, maybe she was raised that way."

"That's not a thing, Mom."

"It *is* a thing, son. It would be nice if girls weren't so aggressive."

Though it was just the beginning of their relationship, I was rooting for her already.

"We'll see where it goes."

Following graduation, Alexander needed to find new living arrangements.

"Sean is actually renting a room in his apartment."

"Who's Sean again?"

"He's the guy who moved to Nashville to start the college men's ministry."[4]

"Oh, yeah, I remember!"

"I could probably find cheaper, but I don't really want to live with four guys again."

Alexander ended up moving in with Sean. With time, he learned more about his new roommate. Sean was not only starting up college ministry chapters around the country, he was writing men's Bible studies.

I could barely contain my glee.

Alexander yawned again, the fourth time in our current phone conversation.

"Are you sleeping enough?" I asked.

"Yeah, I was just up late talking to Sean."

"Is everything okay?" I hoped that they were getting along.

"Mmm..." Alexander mumbled.

"Hello?"

"Yeah, I just hadn't decided if I was going to talk to you about this."

I wrung my hands. "Is he kicking you out?" Alexander was not a dirty person, but he wasn't the best at picking things up around the house.

"Everything's fine, Mom," he cleared his throat. "Sean and I were just up till 2 a.m. talking about purity."

My eyes nearly popped out of my head.

Breathe.

"Okay." I hoped that my silence would elicit more information. It did not. "So...what do you think?" I dared probe.

"Well, Mom, I don't know how much I want to talk to you about this," he repeated, "but I will say that Sean helped me to think about it a little differently."

Despite what I interpreted as good news, my ego was slightly wounded.

"But your dad and I talked to you about God's plan for intimacy while you were growing up."

"Yeah, but you didn't convince me."

Ouch.

"Well," I sighed, "I'm glad that you were able to talk with Sean about it."

The Lord was so faithful.

A few days later, another conversation.

"How's the book coming along, Mom?"

Though we worked at different genres, writing was an interest that we shared. I loved our chats about lyrics, composition, and fodder for future pieces.

"Oh, it's going," I acknowledged. "I think I'm getting close. I just want to do a good job, Lovey. It's so difficult to put little signs and wonders on paper."

"I'm sure you're doing great," Alexander reassured me. "Send me a chapter or two, I'd love to see it."

"Okay, but I'm not finished, you know! I'm still working on it."

"I get it. I send you work-in-progress stuff all the time."

"Okay. You're right! I will," I agreed.

"Yeah, I was telling my girlfriend about it the other day. She loved the idea. Then, it was crazy, Mom, we were driving and she was telling me how much she enjoyed fall. The leaves are just starting to change color here."

I looked out the window. With so many evergreens, there was little autumn glow as of yet. Alexander continued excitedly.

"We pulled into the grocery store parking lot and right then, before we got out of the car, a *huge*, like, the *epitome* of what you imagine the *perfect* fall leaf looks like, landed right in the middle of the windshield."

How sweet the Lord was.

"I looked at her and said, 'a God wink.'"

He got it!

The Lord was so kind. He had shown so much faithfulness. He had brought about so many answers to prayer.

Case in point: my son was now praying for *me*.

"Amen," Alexander concluded.

"Amen," I whispered, and praised the God who faithfully pursues.

THANKSGIVING

It was early October. Walking quickly across campus in the 38-degree chill, I endeavored to avoid the mist of sprinkler pipes being emptied by maintenance crews. The low growl of compressors signaled the arrival of fall.

My calendar for the day was full of advising meetings with freshmen. The twenty-minute appointments, required for their first-year seminar, were a time to check in with these newest members to the community and ensure their successful transition to college. I always made sure to have tissues and chocolate on hand.

One by one, students would knock gingerly on my door, their questioning faces peering through the glass pane. Upon my signal, they would enter shyly and make their way to the seat across from me. Inevitably, their legs would bang against back metal panel of my desk.

"Oh, I'm sorry!"

"No problem," I would reassure them. "It's just a bad design."

I tried to mix banter with encouragement. My questions aimed to uncover any difficulties they might be experiencing. I asked about classes, tests, roommates. Student who seemed to be struggling academically were quizzed on their study and sleep habits. I always left time at the end to ask if my advisees had any questions. Most did.

"When do we register for spring classes?"

"How do I add a major?"

"Where can I find out more about study abroad?"

"Is it too late to drop a class?"

A beautiful young woman from Mongolia was my last appointment of the day. The only international student in the course that term, Chinua tapped on my door the minute of our scheduled meeting. She wore an olive green turtleneck sweater and dark jeans under a long wool jacket. She looked manicured, refined, chic. As she entered, more warily than most, I thought of the assignments that Chinua had turned in so far—thoughtful, thorough, academically strong. It was a pleasure to have such students.

"I love your coat," I opened, trying to set her at ease.

"Thank you."

Chinua remained standing near the door.

"Please," I gestured to the closest office chair.

Taking a seat, Chinua managed *not* to bang the metal back of my desk. I smiled.

"How are classes going?"

"Fine."

"How about your roommate?"

"I have two."

"Two? In one dorm room?"

"We live in a house off-campus."

Chinua answered my questions politely, succinctly. I was having a hard time eliciting more than a few words for each response. When our volley began to feel more like Twenty Questions than a conversation, I decided to invite Chinua to direct the remainder of our exchange.

"Do you have any questions for me, Chinua?"

"I *do*." She sounded relieved.

The young woman scooted forward in her seat. In her right hand, she lifted a small index card. A list.

"Go ahead," I prompted. "What are your questions?"

Chinua's expression had become intense—or was it emotional? I began to worry that something bad had happened. Her eyes were glued to the note card in her hand.

"Mmm..." she began shyly. "How do I make friends with American students?"

I was taken aback. Class schedules, study techniques, transfer credits... these were the issues about which I generally advised.

The matter of friendship was new territory. My mind raced in a dozen directions.

Was this related to her shyness? Her off-campus residency? In a dorm on-campus she would've been in more regular contact with a plethora of students. *Was it a cultural issue? Or was she just homesick?*

Chinua's gaze had fallen to her lap. She looked ashamed.

"Oh, Chinua," I began. "Friendships take time."

She nodded.

"Have you joined any clubs?"

"The ballroom dance club."

"That sounds fun."

Chinua batted her eyes in acknowledgment.

"What about your roommates?"

"One is a junior and one is a senior. They already have friends."

I considered contacting the Campus Life people to talk about housing assignments.

"I'm sorry if they're not reaching out, Chinua," I sympathized. I thought of the other students who had entered my office that day—and the three who had forgotten about their appointments and needed to be sent email reminders. They, too, were lonely and in need of friends. Perhaps they were intimidated by the exoticness and relative sophistication of this international student. Perhaps they didn't know how to start a conversation with someone from a country that they might not be able to locate on a map.

Chinua waited attentively for some advice, some suggestion, some help. I sighed.

"Most first-year students are feeling the same things you are, Chinua. Some people are just better at hiding it." The young woman looked at me curiously, as if she could not imagine such a thing. "I would encourage you to be proactive, seek out people that you'd like to know. Ask to sit with someone in the cafeteria, or invite a classmate to study with you..." It wasn't much, but it was a start.

Chinua nodded. She had a plan.

My advisee looked down again to her list. She pushed aside a wisp of shiny, black hair. Again, she awaited my cue.

"Do you have more questions?"

"Yes," she admitted, clearing her throat discreetly. "Mmm... How often should we give things to people?"

"What do you mean?"

"Mmm," she considered, looking up. Evidently, she would have to go off script. "One of my roommates left me a note and some candy."

"That was very nice."

"Is that not normal?"

What was "normal?" Was giving gifts "normal?" Was not giving gifts "normal?"

155

It was always enlightening to catch a glimpse of the world through a new lens.

"It is not *expected* that you give gifts to your roommates," I explained.

"So, she didn't have to do that?" Chinua sounded excited.

"No," I shook my head. "She didn't have to do that. It was a nice gesture."

We sat for a moment in silence, savoring the thought of a relative stranger spending time and money to show kindness to another human being. It was thoughtful, amiable, even bounteous. It was also, potentially, a nascent sign of friendship.

A timid smile lifted Chinua's countenance.

The room felt lighter.

"Do you have any other questions for me, Chinua?"

"One more." She looked down again as if to check the wording recorded on the page.

"Mmm...Thanksgiving is on the calendar next month."

"Yes."

"What is the right thing to do?"

"What do you mean?"

My mind conjured our family tradition of taking turns around the table saying things for which we were thankful.

Where would Chinua spend the holiday? I thought of the blessing that Darlene's invitation had been to me as a college freshman and wondered if the International Student Center would organize something for these visitors to the U.S.

Would someone invite Chinua?

Should I invite Chinua?

"Mmm...," Chinua endeavored to reformulate her query. "How should, how do I show thanks to the people around me?"

Another lens. A fresh perspective.

A new tradition for me.

A HEAVENLY PERSPECTIVE

It was the weekly gathering of faithful ladies in the neighborhood. The instigator: 92-year-old Mirriam. Among the first of the neighbors we had met upon arriving on our street, Mirriam had brought us a basket of goodies and her well-wishes. She had also invited us to church. Though now mostly confined to her home, Mirriam continued her ministry of prayer, exhortation, and encouragement to any who would cross her threshold—family, caretakers, friends, and neighbors alike. I looked forward to the eclectic and unexpected group of women who might show up any given week to be blessed by her company.

There were four of us in attendance that day. Mirriam sat in her usual Victorian-style armchair across from the upright piano. Two heirloom clocks sat atop its wooden frame. The side table adjacent to Mirriam bore an antique lamp, a landline telephone, and several devotional books. Next to this, a sofa sat in front of a large bay window framed by delicate draperies. Two neighbor ladies had pushed aside several throw pillows and more devotional books to sit atop its flowered upholstery. A veteran attendee, I had taken the liberty of moving an armchair from its designated spot in front of the oak bowed glass china cabinet filled with tea cups of a distinctly feminine character. Now in the middle of the sitting room, I faced the group of ladies while enjoying the view of Mirriam's front yard. There, shrouded from the street by lilac bushes, holly, aspen, and pine, one could rest on a garden bench next to a natural spring and admire a spectacular purple clematis on a trellis garden arch while keeping time on a cast-iron sundial. It was delightful.

Among other important petitions, we had been praying for the daughter of one neighbor who was engaged to a man antagonistic to the Christian faith. Nia tearfully recounted the most recent revelations: the fiancé's avoidance of Nia and her husband because of their beliefs, his expectation that they not ever discuss their faith in his presence, and his recent declaration that his future children—Nia's grandchildren—would not be allowed to spend time with her and her husband. Nia was devastated. We were all devastated. All, it seemed, except Mirriam.

Our hostess cocked her snowy head to the side, as if listening for the voice of her Maker.

"Nia," Mirriam began compassionately, "I want to tell you a story."

I moved the throw pillow from behind my lower back and leaned more comfortably into Mirriam's cushioned armchair. *What would this sweet saint have to offer our dear sister?*

"I was a naughty young woman," Mirriam began. "I was far from the Lord." She took pauses between sentences to catch her breath. "I was engaged to one man and in love with his brother."

"Mirriam, I'm not sure we should be hanging out with you," I teased. Mirriam covered her mouth and batted her beautiful pale blue eyes, still carefully lined with coal.

"It's true!" she insisted. "I was a spoiled girl."

Warm in the toasty house, I removed my cardigan.

"But my husband, Dale," she breathed deeply, "he wouldn't have been attracted to a good girl." She shook her head, remembering. "We were married for nearly 50 years and most of the time it was like this." She tapped her knuckles together, a show of quarrels and strife.

I tried to imagine Mirriam fighting with anyone and could not. Her strength and spunk were exceeded only by her pliability and submissiveness to the Lord's will.

Looking around, I realized that I had never seen a picture of Mirriam's late husband. This, despite the fact that her walls and side tables were covered with photos of her children, grandchildren, and great-grandchildren. I had even seen school pictures of sundry neighbor kids. But no Dale. No Mirriam and Dale. Why hadn't I noticed it before?

Mirriam and I had talked about him. I remembered a conversation that we had shared years earlier while doing a Bible study together. Mirriam had encouraged me then to entrust my husband to the Lord, "Don't nag and whine to him, dear. Pray for him!" she had said. She had then told me about how she had waited for years for her unbelieving husband to allow her to tithe. Finally, after oodles of prayer but no nagging, he had acquiesced.

Such a wise woman, Mirriam.

"I eventually came to know the Lord," Mirriam continued. "Hallelujuah!" She raised her hands in worship. I noticed that her ring finger still bore a wedding band.

"Praise God!" we echoed heartily.

"I maybe would not have come to know the Lord without the hardship."

We pondered this as Mirriam caught her breath.

Was this the lesson that she was trying to impart? That Nia's daughter would be, could be, sanctified or brought closer to God through the trials of marriage? That certainly was true in my case. But was it enough to console Nia for the potential estrangement of her daughter and future grandchildren?

I struggled with this sugggestion.

"The Lord is faithful!" Mirriam reminded us, her voice full of conviction. "Dale, that hardened man, Dale finally accepted the Lord." Breath. "At the hospital." Breath. "On his deathbed."

I sat there quietly, still trying to decipher the crux of her story and its relevance to Nia.

Mirriam looked at us hopefully, awaiting our understanding of her message. She found none. Our spiritual mother would have to spell it out.

Leaning forward in her seat, Mirriam enlightened us: "Maybe that was the reason for it all."

A soul saved.

MIRACLES

Dreading our first Thanksgiving without Alexander and Emily, I was grateful for my aunt and uncle's invitation to join them and their adult children in Colorado. A seventeen hour car ride one way—barring winter road closures in Wyoming—seemed preferable to the loneliness of our family table bereft of offspring. My brother and his kids also agreed to attend.

"Is this it?" Daniel asked as we idled on the rural street before a well-lit rancher.

"I'm not sure," I confessed, unable to find the street number on the curbside mailbox. "I haven't been here since I was 15."

"Well, the directions on the phone seem to think this is the place," Daniel concluded, fatigued from the long journey and anxious to escape the car. "We'll know soon enough."

Tiny snow crystals swirled in the icy air as our headlights turned into the driveway. With fresh snow coating the mature landscaping of the acre lot, it looked like a winter wonderland. The flickering glow of candles beckoned us inside.

Our hosts greeted us warmly and gave us a tour of their beautiful home, explaining the many improvements my uncle had made since my last visit.

We admired the renovated kitchen, remodeled master bedroom, tricked out game room filled with collectables. Soon my brother and his crew arrived, and then, my aunt and uncle's kids. Cousin Kay caught us up on her job as an elementary school teacher. Cousin Riley proudly introduced us to his fiancée, Anne, seven months pregnant with their first child.

"Now *you guys* will be the big cousins!" my aunt explained to my nieces and nephew.

The cycle of life.

My brother's children had been only five, eight, and eleven when their mother died—having suffered with illness for five years before that. Such a tragedy.

"So where are you thinking for college?" Kay and I grabbed the eldest. The others headed to the garage to check out my uncle's latest car renovation.

"I'm not sure," Lonni hedged, "but I think I'd like to stay in the Northwest."

Close to her siblings. Close to her dad.

"That would be nice."

Her almond green eyes were pensive, nostalgic.

"Big events and changes always make me miss my mom," she confided.

"Oh, I know, Honey," I sighed, eyes misty.

"I just wish I could share it with her."

We reached for her and the three of us rocked gently together on the couch.

At last, Lonni pulled away, shook her long blonde mane as if to break the spell.

"It's funny how weeks can go by when I don't think about her and then, all of a sudden, I can't stop thinking about her."

We nodded. Kay rubbed her back.

"I have so many good memories of your mom," I offered. She and my brother had been high school sweethearts.

"I would love to hear some," Lonni urged.

"I met her when I was seventeen, just about the age that you are now."

I realized then that there were many things about my sister-in-law that I should share with her children now that they were older. In that moment, I chose a detail that seemed fitting given Lonni's chapter of life.

"Your mom loved learning," I began. "If I read an interesting book, she wanted to talk about it. She wasn't planning on going to college at first but then just wanted to learn more."

Lonni's expression was focused. "I do remember that she loved books."

"She was always so curious, asking questions," I continued.

"That sounds like *you*, Lonni," Kay said.

Lonni smiled faintly.

"You think?"

"Yes, it does," I affirmed, squeezing her hand.

We sat for a moment in silence. The dong of a grandfather clock that had once decorated my grandmother living room signaled half past the hour.

"What's something that you remember about your mom?"

Lonni closed her eyes. A gentle flush warmed her cheeks as she straightened her lithe frame. Then, with gravity and solemnity, she shared a blessed recollection.

"My mom told me that I was *very* special." Her face shone with assurance.

My heart swelled.

"You *are*, sweetheart," Kay nodded, pushing a wisp of her own thick blonde hair behind her ear. "You are."

Thursday morning, I arose to find my uncle refilling the birdfeeder on the back deck. No sooner had he turned to come back inside than a dozen winged warblers alighted on the tray-style feeder—blue jays and starlings and finches. Their colorful feathers illuminated the otherwise pallid landscape.

"You're sure popular," I teased as he closed the back door.

"I do feed them every morning. I guess I buy their affection."

We gazed out the window to take in the show.

"See how the blue jays scare away the smaller birds?" my uncle observed.

"You remind me of Grandma!" I laughed.

My uncle nodded sheepishly. "I guess I do."

Little by the little, the others arose and the house came to life. Nibbling on toast and fruit while the television flashed images of the Macy's Thanksgiving Day parade, Auntie and I gave 15-year-old Shae advise (that she insisted she didn't need) about peer pressure and boys. There were family pictures and games, food prep and a frolic around the neighborhood in the snow. We embraced the craziness that is family.

Before dinner, we loaded into cars so that Riley could show us his own home, just a few miles down the road. My 31-year-old cousin proudly led us through each room. With detail and enthusiasm, Riley narrated the improvements that he had made to his manor—trees planted, back deck built, garage equipped with a lift for his own automobile collection. Amid racecar posters and model cars and other virile embellishments, Riley seemed most pleased with the final room of the tour: the newly-inaugurated nursery.

Returned to my aunt and uncle's home, Anne made gravy and Kay and I set the table while our busy bee hostess administered the final preparations. Finally, the centerpiece—a tree bearing tags commemorating things for which we were thankful—was set aside and the eleven of us sat down to the Thanksgiving feast.

"I made a game for us to play while we're eating," Auntie declared, passing each of us a card with a question on it.

"So like, I'm supposed to answer this question?" Shae asked.

"First read the question out loud." Auntie looked around the table. "Let's see.... Originally, I was going to have everyone answer—but that might take too long. Let's have three people answer each question."

So around the table we went.

"If you could meet anyone, living or dead, who would it be?"

"Elvis!"

"Abraham Lincoln."

"My mom."

"If you could travel anywhere, where would you go?"

"London."

"Greece."

"Hawaii."

It was now Daniel's turn. He donned his reading glasses and lifted the paper to read the pretty script. "What would you do if you won the lottery?"

My husband paused for only a second before answering.

"I would build Bendi a house on the lake."

"Aww...," I cooed. "Thank you, Love."

"And you?" Kay turned to me.

"I'd build a house on the lake," I admitted.

There was a low murmur.

"Well, it sounds like plan," my uncle concluded.

Daniel looked around the table to select a final responder of this question.

"What about you, KC?"

Our 12-year-old nephew appeared to have thought about his answer for some time. His eyes widened, his arms gesticulated, his voice raised.

"*I* would build a place like Disneyland—except it would be where *Jesus* lived. I'd call it 'BC.'"

Our nephew went on to describe an amusement park where people could learn about God. They could see Moses part the Red Sea. They could watch Jesus walk on water. They could fish with Peter and the other disciples. They could witness the Lord's death on the cross....

"People could stay there for three weeks," KC continued. "They could choose where they wanted to go and what they wanted to see and ask questions when they didn't understand."

"Wow, KC," Riley exclaimed, "when did you get so into *Jesus*?"

"I dunno." KC seemed frustrated by the interruption.

"He's talked about this before," Shae quipped.

The room grew quiet, reverent.

KC resumed.

"Everyone would be in costume, so you wouldn't know who was an actor and who was visiting."

"Would *you* be an actor there?" I asked, still trying to get my head around his vision.

"No!" KC insisted. "I don't want to be an actor!" He looked around the table incredulously, as if he couldn't understand why we couldn't see it. "I just love Jesus."

A sacred revelation, indeed.

With dinner finished, we began the task of clearing the table. Loading dishes into the dishwasher, I noticed a framed quote in the kitchen: "Miracles are not contrary to nature. They are only contrary to what (we think) we know about nature. -Augustine."

"I love this," I remarked to my aunt.

"I do, too."

I thought of the efforts that everyone had made for us to be together. Gas and time and meals and new hide-a-bed couches. Between the distance and perils of winter driving and the hassle of hosting such a large crew, our lively reunion would be unjustifiable in a cost-benefit analysis.

I thought of my brother who, following the loss of his wife, had been left to raise three children alone. And yet, here they were nearly seven years later—happy and resilient and unified. A beautiful family.

I thought of Riley and his fiancée and their baby on the way. Was it time or love and responsibility that made of a boy, a man?

I thought of the legacy of a mother's words, the kindredness of kin, the selflessness of love, and God's revelation to a young boy's heart.

Miracles all.

ANSWERS

Summertime meant that I was again able to help in women's ministry at church. I loved Bible studies. I loved ladies. Facilitating the Bible-centered conversations and prayer time of a small group of women was for me both an honor and a blessing.

The current study was one by Laura Dingman: *I Am Found: Quitting the Game of Hide and Seek with God and Others*, an inspiring book about overcoming shame in light of God's love for us. We renewed our minds with Scripture about our redeemed identity in Christ.

Women were going through some heavy stuff. One was moving toward divorce; a second, still healing from a husband's infidelity with her former best friend; a third, praying for wisdom regarding her husband's unexplained seizures. There were other matters as well—the fatigue of mothering young children, the transition to an empty nest, difficult in-laws, financial challenges—all real and onerous and common to life this side of Glory. We prayed for our husbands, our children, our in-laws. We prayed for healing—emotional and physical. We comforted and encouraged each other with God's promises. It felt good to know that we were not alone in our struggles.

Our church was growing and I had been asked to be on the lookout for new facilitators—women with kind hearts who were both familiar with the Scriptures and able to lead. It was a commitment of time and energy that many were unwilling or unable to make.

"I wouldn't know how to do that!"

"I can't promise to be there every week."

"I just don't have the time."

That session, an unusual number of women seemed to have the requisite qualities. Shannon was one. She spoke with gentleness and grace, shared with transparency and discretion, prayed with earnestness and compassion. And while Shannon was familiar with the Scriptures, she also knew that "knowledge puffs up while love builds up."[1] She was one intent on building. Her sister-in-law, Kaleigh, was another. A woman after God's own heart, Kaleigh was kindhearted and humble, astute and wise. More often than not, it was these two servants who remained after class to help me clean up. They were treasures.

My only reluctance in inviting these women to serve was their current chapter in life. Shannon had three young children and a husband who ran a successful—and busy—company. Kaleigh also had young children and a husband, Shannon's brother, who was dealing with health issues. Given their apparent love for one another, I wondered if they might be willing to serve together, wondered if a tag-team might be a solution for the inevitable occasional unavailability of these busy mothers of young children.

Having just pushed the last folded table into the hallway, I dared broach the subject.

"I wanted to ask you guys something," I began. The other women had gone off to pick up children or otherwise take on the day. Directing us to a neighboring classroom, I gently closed the door and turned to face these sweet souls.

"You guys are both such great contributors to our conversations. You're friendly and thoughtful and sensitive to the other ladies..."

They smiled at the compliments, shook their heads gently in protest.

"I know you're busy with young kids and other things," I looked to one of them and then the other, "but I wondered if you would consider facilitating future ladies' Bible studies *together*."

The idea registered in their eyes. Shannon and Kaleigh looked at each other, as if to gauge the other's interest—or lack thereof. The room was silent.

"Please don't feel obligated," I interjected clumsily, knowing that Shannon was relatively new to the church, and that Kaleigh was burdened not only with worry for her husband but also with the additional physical responsibilities of his ailing health.

They asked a bit about what was expected. I blathered about the life-giving nature of the task. They vowed to pray about it. I reiterated my confidence in their ability to lead women well. At last, we hugged goodbye and they ran off to fetch their children.

A few days later, Kaleigh texted the group to inform us that the tests had come back on her husband's MRI. He had a brain tumor. She requested our prayers. The ladies replied with words of faith, messages of hope, gestures of love. I joined my sisters in Christ in prayer for Kaleigh and her husband and wondered if we would ever see her again in class.

These women's plates were full, I decided; their challenges, enough for the season. I determined to never pester them again with such requests.

The following Tuesday, I was still setting up when Shannon arrived.

"Good morning!" I leaned in for a quick hug.

"Oh Bendi!" she cried, setting her things on the table. "I had to come early to tell you." Her eyes glowed with fervency.

"Is everything okay?" I thought of her brother, Kaleigh's husband, and of all that was before them.

Shannon nodded. She was shaking.

"It's not that," she said. "It's about what you asked us last week..."

"Oh, it's okay, Shannon," I interrupted, regretting the pressure that I had evidently put on her with my request. "I understand. You guys have a lot going on right now."

"No, wait!" Shannon insisted, touching my arm. "Let me explain." She took a big breath.

I waited.

"I've been leading at Bible Study Fellowship for years," she began.

"That's wonderful. I've heard it's a great program." So that explained her biblical knowledge.

"It is!" she replied. "It is. But I've been feeling the Lord move me away from that. I felt like He had something else for me."

I could sense my heart grow expectant.

"I'd been praying about how to get plugged in *here*, Bendi, at *this* church," Shannon concluded, her tone exultant. "I would *love* to help with women's ministry! What you asked last week, it was an *answer to prayer!*"

GIVING

"How's the book coming, Mom?"

"Oh, fine, I think. I have thirty-eight chapters now."

"That's great!"

"Yeah... but I'm so close. I feel like I should have forty." A good, round number. The number of days of the flood. The number of days that Moses met with God on Mount Zion. The number of years that the Israelites wandered in the desert before entering the Promised Land. The number of days that Jesus fasted before commencing his ministry. The number of weeks of pregnancy...

"Well, maybe this is something that you would want to include."

I smiled as I sat down on the couch. It warmed my heart to know that our son was looking for signs of the Lord's kindness.

God was so good.

Daisy stood up from her pad behind the desk and lumbered over to plop down at my feet. I leaned down to scratch behind her ears.

"Do tell."

"So, I've been able to put away almost a thousand dollars every month," Alexander began.

"That's wonderful, Honey!"

Our son had been saving for a car. For while SallyAnn the Suburban was still running, her age was catching up with her. She had needed a new fuel pump a year earlier and just a month before, some electrical repairs. Though Daniel was sure that our old rig could capably carry our firstborn for another few years, Alexander was anxious to trade in the no-A/C-missing-side-mirror-two-hundred-sixty-thousand-mile-beast for something a bit more spry.

"I don't know what happened but this month I wasn't able to save anything. I was looking at my expenses and there just wasn't anything left."

"That's okay," I assured him. "You'll get there."

"Well, then it was time to tithe. I was debating doing it."

"The Lord provides, Lovey."

"I know He does, Mom, but three hundred dollars is a lot of money."

"It is." I bit my lip.

"But then I thought about how He has blessed me with health, and a job..."

"And every breath you take!"

Daisy lifted her head to check on me. Softening my tone, I continued: "He says in Malachi 3 that He'll pour out floodgates of blessing if we trust Him in this."

"It's the only place in the Bible that God says to test Him."

My heart swelled. *My son expounding Scripture to me.*

"So?" I prodded at last.

"So, I did it! I sent the money."

"That's great, Alexander. I'm proud of you."

"Yeah. It was the right thing to do."

"It was."

Daisy finally allowed her head to rest again on her front paws. She sighed contentedly. I shifted on the couch and wondered if this was the takeaway: our son's decision to walk in faith. It was, in itself, extraordinary.

But Alexander wasn't finished.

"Then yesterday, Sean brought in the mail."

I leaned forward in my seat.

"And?"

"And I got my tax refund."

"That's wonderful, Lovey! I had forgotten all about that."

"Me too! It was a happy surprise." I could hear the grin in Alexander's voice, teasing me with suspense. "Eight hundred and eighty-five dollars."

My heart leapt with joy.

His mercies never come to an end.[1]

"I will definitely have to write about that."

REVELATION

The thought had been rolling around my head for years. *Had this been the sound of God's "voice"? Would I ever "hear" it clearly this side of Glory?* I had wanted—I had felt compelled—to record stories of God's goodness, his kindness, even his sense of humor. The faithful witness of Jay and Joan, the bold evangelism of Michael, these had been significant examples, nearly tangible evidences to which I could point. The daily signs and wonders, the answered prayers, the providential coincidences, these would be more difficult to put to words.

It had been with both trepidation for my inadequacies and confidence in God's grace that I finally began to write.

Cautiously, I had started to share these efforts with a few friends and family members. In a way, telling people about the idea obliged me to continue. Like signing up for a race or committing aloud to attend a niece's school performance, talking about it was a step toward the goal.

Most had reacted with skepticism. My work-in-progress explanation about "a book devoted to little miracles—in my life, though the goal was to encourage others to recognize the miracles in theirs—and the unique ways that God blesses us" had elicited muted enthusiasm. In fact, more often than not, it had been a great conversation ender.

"Mmm..."

"Okay."

"Let me know how it goes!"

If I hadn't even been able explain it to friends, how would I convince strangers?

Were people even interested—would people *believe*—in a God of miracles?

And who would think I was just crazy?

It was the week before classes were to recommence at Whitworth. Grabbing a coffee between faculty meetings, I ran into Adam of Nashville-waiter fame. We talked briefly about our families, our summer activities.

"And what are you currently working on?" Adam asked, referring to my scholarly pursuits.

What would I tell him? My mind raced. I could tell him that this summer I had worked on a chapter about Christian foreign language pedagogy. Or I could mention the curriculum project for third-year French that I had recently submitted to a publisher. Or I could talk about the conference presentation on the subject of food and female protagonists that I intended to rework into a journal article. But these scholastic activities were not the current focus of my attention.

What would an academic think about vignettes of the Lord's goodness? I wondered.

"Well," I confessed, "I'm actually working on a nonacademic book." Then I tried, again, to communicate the general vision for my manuscript (to give God credit), the heart of my project (to give Him glory).

"I'm trying to write about the little miracles, Adam," I said, "the ways that He blesses us individually and uniquely."

Quietly, Adam pondered my words. All around us, faculty members mingled affably. The growing line for coffee pushed us away from the stir sticks and cream. Nervously awaiting Adam's reaction, I began to think that I had effectively ended yet another exchange. I even considered excusing myself to avoid his reaction altogether.

"But Bendi," Adam finally found the words. "Isn't it all miracles?"

I paused, considered.

"Yes!"

The universe, the perfect conditions for life on earth, the first and second laws of thermodynamics, Daniel's unwavering devotion, gravity, the human genome, the paradox of phytoplankton, Emily's vision of God's Kingdom, synchronous fireflies, the migration of the Monarch butterfly, hummingbirds, the Lord's faithful pursuit of Alexander, love, altruism, sacrifice, divine appointments, friendship, kindness, beauty, answered prayers, joy, laughter...

"Yes," I repeated. "It truly is."

We simply need eyes to see.

EPILOGUE:
BLESSINGS

The alarm cut through the dark fog of sleep.

Two more minutes, I decided, tapping my phone to silence its cry. I wanted to linger in this delightful den just two more minutes.

The heater creaked and groaned as it pushed the chill from the air inside our bedroom. Our faithful four-legged companion wheezed steadily from her newest station on the floor to my right. Then the man I had loved for twenty-eight years—imperfectly and with varying degrees of self-sacrifice—moved closer to take my hand.

"Dear Lord," Daniel whispered, his voice low and husky, "thank You for your faithfulness."

"Amen."

I placed a soft kiss on his cheek before rolling regretfully to my feet. The floorboard moaned under my weight.

"Do you have time for a short run this morning?"

"Sure," I replied.

Steady legs carried me down the stairs where the ambrosial odor of dark roast wafted from the coffee maker. Above the coughs of the travailing pot, the piercing two-note whistle of a black-capped chickadee consecrated the dawn. Then through the kitchen window, I took in the purple glow of the horizon announcing the sun's imminent entrance into the celestial sphere.

A new day.

ENDNOTES

Eyes to See

[1] Acts 10

[2] John 13:23, 19:26, 20:2, 21:7, 21:10, 21:24

[3] This idea was presented by Don Lynn at Heart of the City Church in Coeur d'Alene, Idaho, 2015.

[4] James 1:17

Of Eunuchs and Freshman Rejoicing

[1] Isaiah 53:5-7

[2] John 1:1

[3] Romans 12:1

[4] Acts 8:26-36

[5] Acts 8:39; names altered.

Blessed

[1] Jeremiah 29:11

Sweet Mercy

[1] Isaiah 6:1-8

Life in Color

[1] 2 Corinthians 3:14

[2] Matthew 13:1-23

[3] Jeremiah 51:15

[4] Psalm 95:3-4

Sneaking Out 2.0

[1] Ecclesiastes 4:9-12

We Can Make Our Plans

[1] Proverbs 16:9

[2] Job 9:8-10

[3] John 1:5

[4] Lamentations 3:23

Deception

[1] Genesis 3:8-9 (NLT)

[2] Genesis 3:10 (NLT)

[3] Genesis 3:11 (NLT)

[4] Genesis 3:13 (NLT)

Tree of Life

[1] Proverbs 15:4

"A Good Day for Me"

[1] I Kings 17:7-24

Planning Funerals

[1] Ecclesiastes 7:2

[2] A reference to the previous chapter by the same name.

Noël

[1] Revelations 7:9-10

Faith-Filled Prayer

[1] Ephesians 1:15-19

[2] Philippians 1:3-6

[3] Philippians 4:4-7

Iron Sharpens Iron

[1] Proverbs 27:17

A Divine Appointment

[1] Real Life Ministries, Post Falls, ID. www.
RealLifeMinistries.com

[2] Acts 20:35

Preach!

[1] Matthew 7:3-5

Known and Loved

[1] Matthew 10:29

[2] Matthew 10:31 (NKJV)

[3] Luke 12:7 (ESV)

Waiting Tables in Nashville

[1] Singer, songwriter PIERRE (Instagram @pierre-
music.official)

Unfailing Kindness

[1] Jeremiah 31:3

[2] Psalm 34:8

[3] *BUD Ministries.* BUD Ministries, Inc., 2017.
www.budministries.com.

[4] Ibid.

Answers
[1] I Corinthians 8:1

Giving
[1] Lamentations 3:22 (ESV)

ABOUT THE EDITORS

Hannah Mumm is an undergraduate student at Whitworth University in Spokane, Washington, majoring in English and French.

Madison Smoak is an undergraduate student in Santa Barbara, CA. A rising senior, she studies English and Spanish at Westmont College. She enjoys writing for the Westmont *Horizon Newspaper* and *Network'd Magazine*.